GATHER ROUND ME

GATHER ROUND ME

THE BEST OF IRISH POPULAR POETRY

Edited by Christopher Cahill

BEACON
150

BEACON PRESS

BOSTON

BEACON PRESS
25 Beacon Street
Boston, Massachusetts 02108 – 2892
www.beacon.org

Beacon Press books are published under the auspices of
the Unitarian Universalist Association of Congregations.

Printed in the United States of America

09 08 07 06 05   8 7 6 5 4 3 2 1

This book is printed on acid-free paper that meets the uncoated
paper ANSI / NISO specifications for permanence as revised in 1992.

Text design by Christopher Kuntze
Composed in Miller and Sophia types.

LIBRARY OF CONGRESS CATALOGING-IN-PUBLICATION DATA

Gather round me : the best of Irish popular poetry / edited by Christopher Cahill.
    p. cm.
  ISBN 0-8070-6870-5 (cloth)
  ISBN 0-8070-6873-X (pbk.)
  1. English poetry—Irish authors. 2. Irish Poetry—Translations into English.
  3. Songs, English—Ireland—Texts. 4. Popular literature—Ireland.
  5. Ireland—Poetry. I. Cahill, Christopher. II. Title.
  PR8851.G36 2004
  821.008'09417—dc22   2003021507

This book is for Ben Kiely—
friend and mentor, rake and rambler,
the living embodiment of the traditions
of poetry and song represented
in these pages.

CONTENTS

PART III *HOW THE HEART OF THE MINSTREL IS BREAKING!*

PART IV *I LEAVE MY WARM HEART WITH YOU, THOUGH MY BACK I'M FORCED TO TURN*

Gather round me boys, will yez
Gather round me?
And hear what I have to say,
Before ould Sally brings me
My bread and jug of tay.
I live in Faddle Alley,
Off Blackpits near the Coombe;
With my poor wife called Sally,
In a narrow, dirty room.

Gather round me, and stop yer noise,
Gather round me till my tale is told;
Gather round me, ye girls and ye boys,
Till I tell yez stories of the days of old;
Gather round me, all ye ladies fair,
And ye gentlemen of renown;
Listen, listen, and to me repair,
Whilst I sing of beauteous Dublin town.

ZOZIMUS (1794–1846)

INTRODUCTION

In the hallway outside the bedroom I slept in while growing up in my family's apartment in New York City hung a framed poem. Copied out in a calligraphic hand and adorned with a few pale shamrocks, it was entitled "The Exile from Auniskirtane." It was written by John D. Cahill, my father's grandfather, who, at the end of the nineteenth century, had left Auniskirtane, in the Sliabh Luachra area of County Kerry, and come to New York, where he found work "on the cops," as it used to be said. The poem begins like this:

> The river is my playground.
> Low hills look down on me.
> I cannot see a hill or river now
> But I long to cross the sea.
>
> The river flows down the mountain.
> The hills traverse the sky.
> My heart lies on that river
> Until the day I die.

And it goes on for a few more verses. It's not an especially good poem—I much prefer the same great-grandfather's brief memoir that begins, "I was born in a vale. I pity any man that was not born in a vale"—but it held a great allure for me when I was a child, with the hereditary connection it offered to a lost country with a strange name and a lovely, unstable landscape, with hills that were low one moment and traversing the sky (whatever that could mean) the next. And that poem still seems to me to encapsulate a good part of what poetry has meant for the Irish—especially, perhaps, for the emigrant Irish—not only in its themes of exile and loss and nostalgia, but in the idea, clear as my own last name written on that framed sheet of paper, of poetry as a thing one does oneself, a natural response to the sorrows and otherwise of being alive.

The poems and songs brought together in this book are instances of portable art, things made out of words by people who, in many instances, had little else but words. There are a number of types of poems in this book—anonymous broadside ballads (so called because they were printed on one side of a single sheet of paper), folk epigrams, sentimental Victorian verses, poems by "literary" writers working in popular modes, and even rock lyrics—they span over four hundred years, from the seventeenth century through to the twentieth century, and they come not only from Ireland but from across the Irish diaspora in America, Canada, England, and Australia. Despite these varying origins, they can all be seen as parts of a larger common undertaking. The poems gathered here are a sliver of a vast body of material, but I have tried to give a sense of the many ways that writers from a wide variety of circumstances have made from words something that others could have and use and take pleasure from and give to others. These poems are "popular" because, whether or not their authorship is known, they were taken up by and came to belong to the populace. They were passed around and refashioned to varying circumstances and places; anyone who doubts that this is still going on can try searching the Internet for lyrics to songs by the Pogues and see the plenitude of conflicting versions to be found there.

The poet Maire MacEntee once described the Irish-speaking peasantry she grew up among on the Dingle Peninsula in County Kerry as being highly cultured even when illiterate. In the aftermath of the collapse of the Gaelic order in Ireland, which crumbled under a successive wave of calamities—the short list would include the Elizabethan wars, the Flight of the Earls in 1607, the Cromwellian ravagements, the defeat of James II at the Battle of the Boyne in 1690, the Great Famine of the 1840s and the pattern of massive emigration it established, not to mention the failed rebellions of 1798, 1803, and 1848—the writing of poems, which previously had been the province of a highly formal bardic system, fell to the dispossessed, who took up the task for pleasure or from felt necessity. That adherence to verse-making and balladeering as a means of preserving and reconstituting a lost order is present throughout the poems in this book, even when a given author, as in the case of W. B. Yeats, might be highly cultured indeed and a member of that Protestant ascendancy that superseded the Gaelic chieftains.

The poems and songs in *Gather Round Me*, even the laments, were made to be enjoyed, and they are offered here in that spirit. Like one of the great books of Ireland, they move, roughly speaking, through the course of a day and a night. Many of the poems in the middle of the book describe such daytime activities as working the fields or fighting in battle or wandering the countryside, and I've arranged the beginning and end so that one can travel with the whole collection from "the dawning of the day" until "the parting glass." The collection is meant to proceed in a way somewhat akin to a musical performance, with a slow number, a ballad, entering in to put the brakes on a series of fast ones, or livelier poems, with never too much of the same sort of thing all in a row. Certain themes recur. Some of them—war, revelry, the sporting life, nationhood, romantic love, crime and punishment—are universal themes, the sources of poetry and song the world over. Others, though—emigration, for instance, or "exile," as it is often put—seem especially Irish.

The love of place, and the almost ritualistic telling over of place-names—of towns and townlands, rivers and streams, hills and mountains, counties and provinces—is a distinctively Irish concern and one that pervades the whole range of poems in this collection, from a plaintive lament like William Allingham's "The Winding Banks of Erne" to a caustic vituperation like "The Galbally Farmer" to a bittersweet memory piece like Shane MacGowan's "The Broad Majestic Shannon." The Irish language has a word, *dinnseanchas*, that can be roughly translated into English, though there is not really an equivalent concept, as "the lore of place-names." It refers to the way that beliefs and events and episodes of local history came to be embedded in the names of places, and of how that body of knowledge was passed down from one generation to the next—a way of keeping the past alive not only in memory but in the actual inhabited landscape. These names often exist, or once existed, on an almost microscopic level, as can be seen, for instance, in the writer and cartographer Tim Robinson's maps of the Aran Islands, Connemara, and the Burren. On those maps, Irish-language names are recorded for practically every outcropping of stone in that stony west of Ireland landscape—the equivalent might be if someone knew a name for each scuff and scratch on the sidewalks of New York. It seems fitting that the traditions of poem and song in Ireland, and among the Irish worldwide, should be steeped so fully in this tradition.

So, on to the poems, a rattle bag of fun and misery and delight. I have provided endnotes for each one as signposts for those totally unfamiliar with the terrain, but in truth the poems sing themselves without need of explanation. It should be noted, if it cannot be explained, that it was the need that people felt to have these things exist that brought them into being.

Christopher Cahill

PART I

AS I ROVED OUT ON A SUMMER'S MORNING

The Dawning of the Day
"Fainne Geal an Lae"

At early morn I once had been
　　Where Lene's blue waters flow,
When summer bid the groves be green,
　　The lamp of light to glow.
As on by bower, and town, and tower,
　　And widespread fields I stray,
I met a maid in the greenwood shade
　　At the dawning of the day.

Her feet and beauteous head were bare,
　　No mantle fair she wore;
But down her waist fell golden hair,
　　That swept the tall grass o'er.
With milking-pail she sought the vale,
　　And bright her charms' display;
Outshining far the morning star
　　At the dawning of the day.

Beside me sat that maid divine
　　Where grassy banks outspread.
"Oh, let me call thee ever mine,
　　Dear maid," I sportive said.
"False man, for shame, why bring me blame?"
　　She cried, and burst away—
The sun's first light pursued her flight
　　At the dawning of the day.

EDWARD WALSH (1805–1851)

The Colleen Rue

As I roved out on a summer's morning a-speculating most curiously,
To my surprise whom should I spy but a rural maiden approaching me
I stood a while in deep meditation, contemplating what I should do,
Till at last recruiting all my sensations I thus accosted the Colleen Rue.

Are you Aurora or the goddess Flora, Artemidora or Venus bright
Or Helen fair beyond compare, whom Paris stole from the Grecian sight
O fairest creature you have enslaved me, I'm captivated in Cupid's clew
Your golden sayings are infatuations that have ensnared me, a Colleen Rue.

Kind sir, be easy and do not tease me; with your false praises most jestingly
Your dissimulation and invocation are vaunting praises alluring me
I'm not Aurora or the goddess Flora, but a rural maiden to all men's view
Who is here condoling my situation; my appellation—the Colleen Rue.

Oh, were I Hector, that noble victor who died a victim to Grecian skill
Or were I Paris whose deeds are various an arbitrator on Ida's hill
I'd range through Asia, likewise Arabia, Pennsylvania seeking for you
The burning raygions like sage Orpheus to see your face my sweet
      Colleen Rue.

TRADITIONAL (EARLY 19TH CENTURY)

A Vision

The Brightest of the Bright met me on my path so lonely;
    The Crystal of all Crystals was her flashing dark-blue eye;
Melodious more than music was her spoken language only;
    And glories were her cheeks, of a brilliant crimson dye.

With ringlets above ringlets her hair in many a cluster
    Descended to the earth, and swept the dewy flowers;
Her bosom shone as bright as a mirror in its lustre;
    She seemed like some fair daughter of the Celestial Powers.

She chanted me a chant, a beautiful and grand hymn,
    Of him who should be shortly Eire's reigning King—
She prophesied the fall of the wretches who had banned him;
    And somewhat else she told me which I dare not sing.

Trembling with many fears I called on Holy Mary,
    As I drew nigh this Fair, to shield me from all harm,
When, wonderful to tell! she fled far to the Fairy
    Green mansion of Sliabh Luachra in terror and alarm.

O'er mountain, moor, and marsh, by greenwood, lough, and hollow,
    I tracked her distant footsteps with a throbbing heart;
Through many an hour and day did I follow on and follow,
    Till I reached the magic palace reared of old by Druid art.

There a wild and wizard band with mocking fiendish laughter
    Pointed out me her I sought, who sat low beside a clown;
And I felt as though I never could dream of Pleasure after
    When I saw the maid so fallen whose charms deserved a crown.

Then with burning speech and soul, I looked at her and told her
    That to wed a churl like that was for her the shame of shames,

When a bridegroom such as I was longing to enfold her
    To a bosom that her beauty had kindled into flames.

But answer made she none; she wept with bitter weeping,
    Her tears ran down in rivers, but nothing could she say;
She gave me then a guide for my safe and better keeping,—
    The Brightest of the Bright, whom I met upon my way.

Oh, my misery, my woe, my sorrow and my anguish,
    My bitter source of dolor is evermore that she
The loveliest of the Lovely should thus be left to languish
    Amid a ruffian horde till the Heroes cross the sea.

AODHAGAN O'RATHAILLE (1675–1729)
translated from the Irish by James Clarence Mangan

The Old Triangle

A hungry feeling came o'er me stealing
And the mice were squealing in my prison cell,
And that old triangle
Went jingle jangle,
Along the banks of the Royal Canal.

To begin the morning
The warder bawling
Get out of bed and clean up your cell,
And that old triangle
Went jingle jangle,
Along the banks of the Royal Canal.

The screw was peeping
The lag was sleeping
While he lay weeping for the girl Sal,
And the old triangle
Went jingle jangle,
Along the banks of the Royal Canal.

The day was dying and the wind was sighing,
As I lay crying in my prison cell,
And the old triangle
Went jingle jangle,
Along the banks of the Royal Canal.

On a fine spring evening,
The lag lay dreaming
The seagulls wheeling high above the wall,
And the old triangle
Went jingle jangle,
Along the banks of the Royal Canal.

In the female prison
There are seventy women
I wish it was with them that I did dwell,
Then that old triangle
Could jingle jangle
Along the banks of the Royal Canal.

BRENDAN BEHAN (1923–1964)

The Mantle So Green

As I went out walking one morning in June,
To view the fair fields and the meadows in bloom,
I spied a young damsel, she appeared like a queen,
With her costly fine robes and her mantle so green.

I stood with amazement and was struck with surprise,
I thought her an angel that fell from the skies.
Her eyes were like diamonds, her cheeks like the rose,
She is one of the fairest that nature composed.

I said, "My pretty fair maid, if you will come with me
We'll both join in wedlock, and married we'll be,
I'll dress in rich attire, you'll appear like a queen,
With costly fine robes and your mantle so green."

She answered, "Young man, you must me excuse,
For I'll wed with no man, you must be refused,
To the woods I will wander to shun all men's view,
For the lad that I love is in famed Waterloo."

"If you won't marry, tell me your love's name,
For I being in battle, I might know the same."
"Draw near to my garment and there will be seen,
His name all embroidered on my mantle of green."

In raising her mantle there I did behold
His name and his surname were in letters of gold;
Young William O'Reilly appeared to my view,
He was my chief comrade in famed Waterloo.

"We fought so victorious where bullets did fly
In the far field of honour your true love does lie,

We fought for three days till the fourth afternoon,
He received his death-summons on the eighteenth of June.

But when he was dying I heard his last cry,
'If you were here, Lovely Nancy, contented I'd die.'
Now Peace is proclaimed, and the truth I declare,
Here is your love token, the gold ring I wear."

She stood in amazement, then paler she grew,
She flew to my arms with a heart full of woe,
"To the woods I will wander for the lad I adore."
"Rise up, lovely Nancy, your grief I'll remove.

"O, Nancy, dear Nancy, 'tis I won your heart
In your father's garden that day we did part.
Now the wars are all over, no trouble is seen
And I'll wed with my true love in her mantle so green."

TRADITIONAL (19TH CENTURY)

Going to Mass Last Sunday

Going to Mass last Sunday my true love passed me by,
I knew her mind was altered by the rolling of her eye;
And when I stood in God's dark light my tongue could word no prayer
Knowing my saint had fled and left her reliquary bare.

Sweet faces smiled from holy glass, demure in saintly love,
Sweet voices ripe with Latin grace rolled from the choir above;
But brown eyes under Sunday wear were all my liturgy;
How can she hope for heaven who has so deluded me?

When daffodils were altar gold her lips were light on mine
And when the hawthorn flame was bright we drank the year's new wine;
The nights seemed stained-glass windows lit with love that paled the sky,
But love's last ember perishes in the winter of her eye.

Drape every downcast day now in purple cloth of Lent,
Smudge every forehead now with ash, that she may yet repent,
Who going to Mass last Sunday could pass so proudly by
And show her mind was altered by the rolling of an eye.

DONAGH MACDONAGH (1912–1968)

The Fiddler of Dooney

When I play on my fiddle in Dooney,
Folk dance like a wave of the sea;
My cousin is priest in Kilvarnet,
My brother in Mocharabuiee.

I passed my brother and cousin:
They read in their books of prayer;
I read in my book of songs
I bought at the Sligo fair.

When we come at the end of time
To Peter sitting in state,
He will smile on the three old spirits,
But call me first through the gate;

For the good are always the merry,
Save by an evil chance,
And the merry love the fiddle,
And the merry love to dance:

And when the folk there spy me,
They will all come up to me,
With 'Here is the fiddler of Dooney!'
And dance like a wave of the sea.

W. B. YEATS (1865–1939)

The Little Door

I cried last night at the little door in the distance,
And I cried again on the love of my heart, my joy,
Till her mother came and told me over the threshold
She had slipped away in the night with the brownhaired boy.

TRADITIONAL
translated from the Irish by Benedict Kiely

The Forsaken Soldier

When I rose like a Russian that morning,
No cross on my forehead I signed,
For the thought that my true love had left me
It drove me clean out of my mind.
I reached for a scythe that hung high in the hawthorn,
Fell to her with file and blue sharping-stone,
And stripped to the waist in the cornfield
I cut half the harvest alone.

My feet are too long without leather,
My pockets much longer want gold,
I envy the old mountain weather
For his love tales need never be told.
They say that his heartache all winter will tarry
And lead to the tomb before next Easter day,
And the boys that I hurled with will carry
My corpse to its rest in the clay.

If I were stretched prone with the fever
Or seven years under the ground,
And you came to my tomb, love, and called me
I would rise from the dead with one bound.
My sorrow that death did not strike down my father,
'Fore he drove me to drink & the King's own armie,
In the boneyard my hard bed is waiting,
O my darling have pity on me.

HUDIE DEVANEY (1914–1984)
translated from the Irish by Paddy Tunney

The Emigrant's Letter

Dear Danny,
I'm takin' the pen in me hand
To tell you we're just out o' sight o' the land;
    In the grand Allan liner we're sailin' in style,
    But we're sailin' away from the Emerald Isle;
And a long sort o' sigh seemed to rise from us all
As the waves hid the last bit of ould Donegal.
    Och! it's well to be you that is takin' yer tay
    Where they're cuttin' the corn in Creeshla the day.

I spoke to the captain—he won't turn her round,
And if I swum back I'd be apt to be drowned,
    So here I must stay—oh! I've no cause to fret,
    For their dinner was what you might call a banquet.
But though it is 'sumpchus,' I'd swop the whole lot,
For the ould wooden spoon and the stirabout pot;
    And sweet Katty Farrell a-wettin' the tay
    Where they're cuttin' the corn in Creeshla the day!

If Katey is courted by Patsey or Mick,
Put a word in for me with a lump of a stick,
    Don't kill Patsey outright, he has no sort of chance,
    But Mickey's a rogue you might murther at wance;
For Katey might think as the longer she waits
A boy in the hand is worth two in the States:
    And she'll promise to honour, to love and obey
    Some robber that's roamin' round Creeshla the day.

Good-bye to you Dan, there's no more to be said,
And I think the salt wather's got into me head,
    For it dreeps from me eyes when I call to me mind,
    The friends and the colleen I'm leavin' behind;

Oh, Danny, she'll wait; whin I bid her good-bye,
There was just the laste taste of a tear in her eye,
    And a break in her voice whin she said "You might stay,
    But plaze God you'll come back to ould Creeshla some day."

PERCY FRENCH (1854–1920)

The Small Towns of Ireland

Public houses in Irish country towns are very often general merchants as well. You drink at a counter with bacon on it. Brooms and plastic dustpans hang from the ceiling. Loaves of new bread are stacked on top of fuse wire and, over all, there is a deep, delicious silence that can be found only in Ireland, in the midlands of Ireland in particular— the least touristed and profoundest part of that whole sad, beautiful country. Much that is native and traditional goes on, including the printing of ballads in metres derived from the Celts via Tom Moore. These ballads are called hedge poetry and their authors are the last descendants of the Gaelic bards. It was in just such a general shop as I have described that I might have found, pinned up among the notices for a local Feis, Gaelic football matches and Government proclamations, the following ballad, printed on emerald paper in a border of shamrocks.

The small towns of Ireland by bards are neglected,
　　They stand there, all lonesome, on hilltop and plain.
The Protestant glebe house by beech trees protected
　　Sits close to the gates of his Lordship's demesne.

But where is his Lordship, who once in a phaeton
　　Drove out twixt his lodges and into the town?
Oh his tragic misfortunes I will not dilate on;
　　His mansion's a ruin, his woods are cut down.

His impoverished descendant is dwelling in Ealing,
　　His daughters must type for their bread and their board,
O'er the graves of his forebears the nettle is stealing
　　And few will remember the sad Irish Lord.

Yet still stands the Mall where his agent resided,
　　The doctor, attorney and such class of men.
The elegant fanlights and windows provided
　　A Dublin-like look for the town's Upper Ten.

'Twas bravely they stood by the Protestant steeple
　　As over the town rose their roof-trees afar.
Let us slowly descend to the part where the people
　　Do mingle their ass-carts by Finnegan's bar.

I hear it once more, the soft sound of those voices,
　　When fair day is filling with farmers the Square,
And the heart in my bosom delights and rejoices
　　To think of the dealing and drinking done there.

I see thy grey granite, O grim House of Sessions!
　　I think of the judges who sat there in state
And my mind travels back to our monster processions
　　To honour the heroes of brave Ninety-Eight.

The barracks are burned where the Redcoats oppressed us,
　　The gaol is broke open, our people are free.
Though Cromwell once cursed us, Saint Patrick has blessed us—
　　The merciless English have fled o'er the sea.

Look out where yon cabins grow smaller to smallest,
　　Straw-thatched and one-storey and soon to come down,
To the prominent steeple, the newest and tallest,
　　Of Saint Malachy's Catholic Church in our town:

The fine architécture, the wealth of mosaic,
　　The various marbles on altars within-
To attempt a description were merely prosaic,
　　So, asking your pardon, I will not begin.

O my small town of Ireland, the raindrops caress you,
　　The sun sparkles bright on your field and your Square
As here on your bridge I salute you and bless you,
　　Your murmuring waters and turf-scented air.

John Betjeman (1906–1984)

Brian O'Linn

Brian O'Linn was a gentleman born,
His hair it was long and his beard unshorn,
His teeth were out and his eyes far in—
"I'm a wonderful beauty," says Brian O'Linn!

Brian O'Linn was hard up for a coat,
He borrowed the skin of a neighboring goat,
He buckled the horns right under his chin—
"They'll answer for pistols," says Brian O'Linn!

Brian O'Linn had no breeches to wear,
He got him a sheepskin to make him a pair,
With the fleshy side out and the woolly side in—
"They are pleasant and cool," says Brian O'Linn!

Brian O'Linn had no hat to this head,
He stuck on a pot that was under the shed,
He murdered a cod for the sake of his fin—
"'T will pass for a feather," says Brian O'Linn!

Brian O'Linn had no shirt to his back,
He went to a neighbor and borrowed a sack,
He puckered a meal-bag under his chin—
"They'll take it for ruffles," said Brian O'Linn!

Brian O'Linn had no shoes at all,
He bought an old pair at a cobbler's stall,
The uppers were broke and the soles were thin—
"They'll do me for dancing," said Brian O'Linn!

Brian O'Linn had no watch for to wear,
He bought a fine turnip and scooped it out fair,

He slipped a live cricket right under the skin—
"They'll think it is ticking," says Brian O'Linn!

Brian O'Linn was in want of a brooch,
He stuck a brass pin in a big cockroach,
The breast of his shirt he fixed it straight in—
"They'll think it's a diamond," says Brian O'Linn!

Brian O'Linn went a-courting one night,
He set both the mother and daughter to fight—
"Stop, stop," he exclaimed, "if you have but the tin,
I'll marry you both," says Brian O'Linn!

Brian O'Linn went to bring his wife home,
He had but one horse, that was all skin and bone—
"I'll put her behind me, as nate as a pin,
And her mother before me," says Brian O'Linn!

Brian O'Linn and his wife and wife's mother,
They all crossed over the bridge together,
The bridge broke down and they all tumbled in—
"We'll go home by water," says Brian O'Linn!

TRADITIONAL (EARLY 19TH CENTURY)

My Grief on the Sea

My grief on the sea,
　How the waves of it roll!
For they heave between me
　And the love of my soul!

Abandon'd, forsaken,
　To grief and to care,
Will the sea ever waken
　Relief from despair?

My grief, and my trouble!
　Would he and I were,
In the province of Leinster,
　Or County of Clare!

Were I and my darling—
　O heart-bitter wound!—
On board of the ship
　For America bound.

On a green bed of rushes
　All last night I lay,
And I flung it abroad
　With the heat of the day.

And my Love came behind me,
　He came from the South;
His breast to my bosom,
　His mouth to my mouth.

TRADITIONAL
translated from the Irish by Douglas Hyde

The Brewer's Man

Have I a wife? Bedam I have!
But we was badly mated.
I hit her a great clout one night,
And now we're separated.

And mornin's, going to me work
I meets her on the quay:
'Good mornin' to ye ma'am!' says I:
'To hell with ye!' says she.

L. A. G. STRONG (1896–1958)

The Homeward Bound

Paler and thinner the morning moon grew,
Colder and sterner the rising wind blew;
The pole-star had set in a forest of cloud,
And the icicles crackled on spar and on shroud,
When a voice from below we heard feebly cry:
"Let me see, I shall see my own land ere I die.

"Ah, dear sailor, say, have we sighted Cape Clear?
Can you see any sign? Is the morning light near?
You are young, my brave boy; thanks, thanks for your hand—
Help me up, till I get a last glimpse of the land.
Thank God, 'tis the sun that now reddens the sky;
I shall see, I shall see my own land ere I die.

"Let me lean on your strength, I am feeble and old,
And one half of my heart is already stone-cold.
Forty years work a change! when I first crossed the sea
There were few on the deck that could grapple with me;
But my youth and my prime in Ohio went by,
And I'm come back to see the old spot ere I die."

'Twas a feeble old man, and he stood on the deck,
His arm round a kindly young mariner's neck,
His ghastly gaze fixed on the tints of the east,
As a starveling might stare at the sight of a feast.
The morn quickly rose and revealed to his eye
The land he had prayed to behold, and then die!

Green, green was the shore, though the year was near done;
High and haughty the capes the white surf dashed upon;
A grey ruined convent was down by the strand,
And the sheep fed afar, on the hills of the land!

"God be with you, dear Ireland!" he gasped with a sigh;
"I have lived to behold you—I'm ready to die."

He sank by the hour, and his pulse 'gan to fail,
As we swept by the headland of storied Kinsale;
Off Ardigna Bay it came slower and slower,
And his corpse was clay-cold as we sighted Tramore.
At Passage we waked him, and now he doth lie
In the lap of the land he beheld but to die.

THOMAS D'ARCY MCGEE (1825–1868)

The Drynán Dhun

By road and by river the wild birds sing;
O'er mountain and valley the dewy leaves spring;
The gay flowers are shining, gilt o'er by the sun;
And fairest of all shines the Drynán Dhun.

The rath of the fairy, the ruin hoar,
With white silver splendour it decks them all o'er;
And down in the valleys where merry streams run,
How sweet smell the blossoms of the Drynán Dhun.

Ah! well I remember the soft spring day
I sat by my love 'neath its sweet-scented spray;
The day that she told me her heart I had won,
Beneath the white blossoms of the Drynán Dhun.

The streams they were singing their gladsome song,
The soft winds were blowing the wild woods among,
The mountains shone bright in the red setting sun,
As we sat 'neath the blossoms of the Drynán Dhun.

'Tis my prayer in the morning, my dream at night,
To sit thus again by my heart's dear delight,
With her blue eyes of gladness, her hair like the sun,
And her bright pleasant smile 'neath the Drynán Dhun.

ROBERT DWYER JOYCE (1830–1883)

PART II

THERE WAS WHISKEY ON SUNDAY AND TEARS ON OUR CHEEKS

On Raglan Road
[Air: *The Dawning of the Day*]

On Raglan Road on an autumn day I met her first and knew
That her dark hair would weave a snare that I might one day rue;
I saw the danger, yet I walked along the enchanted way,
And I said, let grief be a fallen leaf at the dawning of the day.

On Grafton Street in November we tripped lightly along the ledge
Of the deep ravine where can be seen the worth of passion's pledge,
The Queen of Hearts still making tarts and I not making hay—
O I loved too much and by such by such is happiness thrown away.

I gave her gifts of the mind I gave her the secret sign that's known
To the artists who have known the true gods of sound and stone
And word and tint. I did not stint for I gave her poems to say.
With her own name there and her own dark hair like clouds over
    fields of May.

On a quiet street where old ghosts meet I see her walking now
Away from me so hurriedly my reason must allow
That I had wooed not as I should a creature made of clay—
When the angel woos the clay he'd lose his wings at the dawn of day.

PATRICK KAVANAGH (1904–1967)

To Inishkea

I'll rise and go to Inishkea,
Where many a one will weep with me—
The bravest boy that sailed the sea
     From Blacksod Bay to Killery.

I'll dress my boat in sails of black,
The widow's cloak I shall not lack,
I'll set my face and ne'er turn back
     Upon the way to Inishkea.

In Arran Island, cold as stone,
I wring my hands and weep my lone
Where never my true love's name was known:
     It were not so in Inishkea.

The friends that knew him there will come
And kiss my cheek so cold and numb.
O comfort is not troublesome
     To kindly friends in Inishkea!

'Tis there the children call your name,
The old men sigh, and sigh the same;
'Tis all your praise, and none your blame,
     Your love will hear in Inishkea.

But you were dear to beast and bird,
The dogs once followed at your word,
Your feet once pressed the sand and sward—
     My heart is sore for Inishkea.

I'll rise and go to Inishkea
O'er many a mile of tossing sea
That hides your darling face from me.
      I'll live and die in Inishkea!

KATHERINE TYNAN-HINKSON (1861–1931)

The Mountain Streams Where the Moorcocks Crow

With my dog and gun o'er yon blooming heather
For recreation I chanced to stray;
Where I espied a charming maiden
And she enticed me a while to stay.
It was many a time I roved with pleasure
To meet my darling on yon moorland plain
Sighing and sobbing and love bewailing,
But now I'm altered in Cupid's chains.

Chorus
Said I, "My charmer, I love you dearly
Tell me your name and your home also"
"Excuse my name and you'll find me dwelling
At the mountain stream where the moorcocks crow."

She said, "Young man I'm going to tell you
Your former folly you must give o'er;
If my parents knew that I'd marry a rover
It's deep affliction I'd undergo.
I'm happy here though I might be married
This two long years and something more
To one superior whom I love dearer
Than the mountain stream where the moorcocks crow.

"So farewell darling, I now must leave you
In hopes to meet you on yon moorland plain,
When I'll discourse a time most charming
So listen to my love-sick tale;
Fare thee well old Ireland, likewise old England,
I leave my darling on the plains below,
May the heavens above protect my love,
At the mountain stream where the moorcocks crow."

TRADITIONAL

From Galway to Graceland

Oh she dressed in the dark and she whispered "Amen"
She was pretty in pink like a young girl again
Twenty years married and she never thought twice
She sneaked out the door and walked into the night
And silver wings carried her over the sea
From the west coast of Ireland to West Tennessee
To be with her sweetheart, oh she left everything
From Galway to Graceland to be with the king

She was humming Suspicion, that's the song she liked best
She had Elvis I Love You tattooed on her breast
When they landed in Memphis, well her heart beat so fast
She'd dreamed for so long, now she'd see him at last
She was down by his graveside day after day
Come closing time they would pull her away
Ah to be with her sweetheart, oh she'd left everything
From Galway to Graceland to be with the king

Ah, they came in their thousands from the whole human race
To pay their respects at his last resting place
Ah, but blindly she knelt there and she told him her dreams
And she thought that he answered or that's how it seems
Then they dragged her away it was handcuffs this time
She said "My good man are you out of your mind.
Don't you know that we're married? See, I'm wearing his ring.
From Galway to Graceland to be with the king.
I come from Galway to Graceland to be with the king."

RICHARD THOMPSON (1949–)

The Fairies

Up the airy mountain,
　Down the rushy glen,
We daren't go a-hunting
　For fear of little men;
Wee folk, good folk,
　Trooping all together;
Green jacket, red cap,
　And white owl's feather!

Down along the rocky shore
　Some make their home,
They live on crispy pancakes
　Of yellow tide-foam;
Some in the reeds
　Of the black mountain lake,
With frogs for their watch-dogs,
　All night awake.

High on the hill-top
　The old King sits;
He is now so old and gray
　He's nigh lost his wits.
With a bridge of white mist
　Columbkill he crosses,
On his stately journeys
　From Slieveleague to Rosses;
Or going up with music
　On cold starry nights,
To sup with the Queen
　Of the gay Northern Lights.

They stole little Bridget
  For seven years long;
When she came down again
  Her friends were all gone.
They took her lightly back,
  Between the night and morrow,
They thought she was fast asleep,
  But she was dead with sorrow.
They have kept her ever since
  Deep within the lake,
On a bed of flag-leaves,
  Watching till she wake.

By the craggy hill-side,
  Through the mosses bare,
They have planted thorn-trees
  For pleasure here and there.
Is any man so daring
  As dig them up in spite,
He shall find the sharpest thorns
  In his bed at night.

Up the airy mountain
  Down the rushy glen,
We daren't go a-hunting
  For fear of little men;
Wee folk, good folk,
  Trooping all together;
Green jacket, red cap,
  And white owl's feather!

WILLIAM ALLINGHAM (1824–1889)

The Hill of Killenarden

Though time effaces memory, and griefs the bosom harden,
I'll ne'er forget, where'er I be, that day at Killenarden;
For there, while fancy revelled wide, the summer's day flew o'er me;
The friends I loved were at my side, and Irish fields before me.

The road was steep; the pelting showers had cooled the sod beneath us;
And there were lots of mountain flowers, a garland to enwreath us.
Far, far below the landscape shone with wheat, and new-mown meadows,
And as o'erhead the clouds flew on, beneath swept on their shadows.

O friends, beyond the Atlantic's foam there may be noble mountains,
And in our new far western home green fields and brighter fountains;
But as for me, let time destroy all dreams, but this one pardon,
And barren memory long enjoy that day on Killenarden.

CHARLES G. HALPINE (1829–1868)

Master McGrath

Eighteen sixty nine being the date of the year,
Those Waterloo sportsmen and more did appear;
For to gain the great prizes and bear them awa',
Never counting on Ireland and Master McGrath.

On the twelfth of December, that day of renown,
McGrath and his keeper they left Lurgan town;
A gale in the Channel, it soon drove them o'er,
On the thirteenth they landed on fair England's shore.

And when they arrived there in big London town,
Those great English sportsmen they all gathered round—
And some of the gentlemen gave a "Ha! Ha!"
Saying, "Is that the great dog you call Master McGrath?"

And one of those gentlemen standing around
Says, "I don't care a damn for your Irish greyhound,"
And another he laughs with a scornful "Ha! Ha!
We'll soon humble the pride of your Master McGrath."

Then Lord Lurgan came forward and said, "Gentlemen,
If there's any among you has money to spend—
For your nobles of England I don't care a straw—
Here's five thousand to one upon Master McGrath."

Then McGrath he looked up and he wagged his old tail,
Informing his lordship, "I know what you mane,
Don't fear, noble Brownlow, don't fear them, agra,
For I'll tarnish their laurels," says Master McGrath.

And Rose stood uncovered, the great English pride,
Her master and keeper were close by her side;

They have let her away and the crowd cried "Hurrah!"
For the pride of all England—and Master McGrath.

As Rose and the Master they both ran along,
"Now I wonder," says Rose, "what took you from your home;
You should have stopped there in your Irish demesne,
And not come to gain laurels on Albion's plain."

"Well, I know," says McGrath, "we have wild heather bogs
But you'll find in old Ireland there's good men and dogs.
Lead on, bold Britannia, give none of your jaw,
Snuff that up your nostrils," says Master McGrath.

Then the hare she went on just as swift as the wind
He was sometimes before her and sometimes behind.
Rose gave the first turn according to law;
But the second was given by Master McGrath.

The hare she led on with a wonderful view.
And swift as the wind o'er the green field she flew.
But he jumped on her back and he held up his paw
"Three cheers for old Ireland," says Master McGrath.

TRADITIONAL (19TH CENTURY)

O'Mahony's Lament

In a foreign land, in a lonesome city,
With few to pity or know or care,
I sleep each night while my heart is burning
And wake each morning to new despair.

Let no one venture to ask my story
Who believes in glory or trusts to fame;
Yes! I have within me such demons in keeping
As are better sleeping without a name.

From many a day of blood and horror,
And night of terror and work of dread,
I have rescued nought but my honour only,
And this aged, lonely, and whitening head.

Not a single hope have I seen fulfilled
For the blood we spilled when we cast the die;
And the future I painted in brightness and pride
Has the present belied and shall still belie.

In this far-off country, this city dreary,
I languished weary, and sad, and sore,
Till the flower of youth in glooms o'er shaded
Grew seared, and faded for evermore.

Oh my land! from thee driven—our old flag furled—
I renounced the world when I went from thee;
My heart lingers still on its native strand
And American land holds nought for me.

Through a long life contriving, hoping, striving,
Driven and driving, leading and led;
I have rescued nought but my honour only
And this aged, lonely and whitening head.

Douglas Hyde (1860–1949)

An Irishman's Dream

Sure I've roamed this wide world over
But of all the lands I've seen
There's no spot I'd rather dwell in
Than my little isle of Green

Only last night I was dreamin'
Of a sight that thrilled me through
But what I saw I'll see no more
'twas too good to be true

Sure the shamrocks were growing on Broadway
Every girl was an Irish colleen
The town of New York was the county of Cork
All the buildings were painted green

Sure the Hudson looked just like the Shannon
Oh, how good and how real it did seem
I could hear me mother singin', sweet Shannon bells ringin'
'twas only an Irishman's dream

JOHN J. O'BRIEN (1916–)

The Mountains of Mourne

Oh, Mary, this London's a wonderful sight,
Wid people here workin' by day and by night:
    They don't sow potatoes, nor barley, nor wheat,
    But there's gangs o' them diggin' for gold in the street—
At least, when I axed them, that's what I was told,
So I just took a hand at this diggin' for gold,
    But for all that I found there, I might as well be
    Where the Mountains o' Mourne sweep down to the sea.

I believe that, when writin', a wish you expressed
As to how the fine ladies in London were dressed.
    Well, if you'll believe me, when axed to a ball,
    They don't wear no top to their dresses at all!
Oh, I've seen them meself, and you could not, in thrath,
Say if they were bound for a ball or a bath—
    Don't be startin' them fashions now, Mary Machree,
    Where the Mountains o' Mourne sweep down to the sea.

There's beautiful girls here—oh, never mind!
With beautiful shapes Nature never designed,
    And lovely complexions, all roses and crame,
    But O'Loughlin remarked wid regard to them same:
"That if at those roses you venture to sip,
The colour might all come away on your lip,"
    So I'll wait for the wild rose that's waitin' for me—
    Where the Mountains o' Mourne sweep down to the sea.

PERCY FRENCH (1854–1920)

The Broad Majestic Shannon

The last time I saw you was down at the Greeks
There was whiskey on Sunday and tears on our cheeks
You sang me a song as pure as the breeze
Blowing up the road to Glenaveigh
I sat for a while at the cross at Finnoe
Where young lovers would meet when the flowers were in bloom
Heard the men coming home from the fair at Shinrone
Their hearts in Tipperary wherever they go

Take my hand, and dry your tears babe
Take my hand, forget your fears babe
There's no pain, there's no more sorrow
They're all gone, gone in the years babe

I sat for a while by the gap in the wall
Found a rusty tin can and an old hurley ball
Heard the cards being dealt, and the rosary called
And a fiddle playing Sean Dun na nGall
And the next time I see you we'll be down at the Greeks
There'll be whiskey on Sunday and tears on our cheeks
For it's stupid to laugh and it's useless to blame
About a rusty tin can and an old hurley ball

So I walked as day was dawning
Where small birds sang and leaves were falling
Where we once watched the row boats landing
By the broad majestic Shannon

SHANE MACGOWAN (1957–)

The County of Mayo

On the deck of Patrick Lynch's boat I sat in woeful plight,
Through my sighing all the weary day, and weeping all the night,
Were it not that full of sorrow from my people forth I go,
By the blessed sun, 'tis royally I'd sing thy praise, Mayo.

When I dwelt at home in plenty, and my gold did much abound,
In the company of fair young maids the Spanish ale went round—
'Tis a bitter change from those gay days that now I'm forced to go
And must leave my bones in Santa Cruz, far from my own Mayo.

They are altered girls in Irrul now; 'tis proud they're grown and high,
With their hair-bags and their top-knots, for I pass their buckles by—
But it's little now I heed their airs, for God will have it so,
That I must depart for foreign lands, and leave my sweet Mayo.

'Tis my grief that Patrick Loughlin is not Earl of Irrul still,
And that Brian Duff no longer rules as Lord upon the hill;
And that Colonel Hugh Mac Grady should be lying dead and low,
And I sailing, sailing swiftly from the county of Mayo.

THOMAS LAVELLE (17TH CENTURY)
translated from the Irish by George Fox

PART III

HOW THE HEART OF THE MINSTREL IS BREAKING!

The Wee Lassie's First Luve

1.

A cannae hear his name an' hide
    My thought wi' ony art;
A cannae see him come, an' calm
    The flitterin' uv my heart;
It's pain tae meet him whun A walk,
    Or meet him nae ava;
A wish him aye tae come tae me,
    A wish him aye awa'.

2.

A dinnae ken what's wrang wi' me;
    A'm vixed, A kennae way;
A cannae talk, A cannae wark;
    My min's a' gang'd agley;
A say sich foolish thin's at whiles
    My face is scorch'd wi' pain . . .
O, let me lave me tae mysel'!
    A jist wud be alane.

3.

A'm nae sae tall as Elsie Barnes,
    A hae nae een like May's,
Yit aft he turns frae May tae me,
    An' ne'er wi' Elsie strays.
A cannae thole tae see him laugh
    Wi' Grace or Rose or Jean,
An' yit he's stan'in' nigh my side
    Mair aft than ony ane.

4.

He's aye sae coorteous, kin', an' free
Wi' mon an' lass an' chiel'
Mayhap he cares nae mair fur me
Than jist tae wish me weel . .
But ah, the kin'ness uv his voice!
An' ah, his dark blue ee!
An' ah, his face an' coortly grace! . .
A think A jist cud dee.

TRADITIONAL

The Street Ballad-Singer's Song (Dan O'Connell)

In the year '44 on the 30th of May
Our brave Liberator these words he did say,
"The time is but short that I have for to stay.
When the locks of my prison shall open
You'll find me so true that the laws I'll obey
And I'll always be so till I'm laid in the clay
For peace is the thing that will carry the day
And bring Parliament back to old Erin."

JEREMIAH O'DONOVAN ROSSA (1831–1915)

Street Ballad

In October 'ninety-seven—
May his soul find rest in heaven—
William Orr to execution was led on.
    The jury, drunk, agreed
    That Irish was his creed;
For perjury and threats drove them on, boys, on,
Here's the memory of the martyr that is gone.

TRADITIONAL (18TH CENTURY)

Rody McCorley

Come tender-hearted Christians all, attention pay to me,
'Till I relate these verses great, these verses two or three,
Concerning of a clever youth who was cut off in his bloom,
And died upon the gallows tree near to the bridge of Toome.

The hero now I speak of, he was proper tall and straight,
Like to the lofty poplar tree his body was complete,
His growth was like the tufted fir that does ascend the air,
And waving o'er his shoulders broad the locks of yellow hair.

In sweet Duneane this youth was born and reared up tenderly,
His parents educated him, all by their industry,
Both day and night they sorely toiled all for their family,
Till desolation it came on by curséd perjury.

'Twas first the father's life they took and secondly the son,
The mother tore her old grey locks, she says "I am undone
They took from me my property, my houses and my land,
And in the parish where I was born I dare not tread upon."

"Farewell unto you sweet Drumaul, if in you I had stayed,
Among the Presbyterians I wouldn't have been betrayed,
The gallows tree I'd ne'er have seen had I remained there
For Dufferin you betrayed me, McErlean you set the snare.

"In Ballyscullion I was betrayed, woe be unto the man,
Who swore me a defender and a foe unto the crown,
Which causes Rody for to lie beneath the spreading thorn,
He'll sigh and say 'Alas the day that ever I was born.'"

Soon young Rody was conveyed to Ballymena town,
He was loaded there with irons strong, his bed was the cold ground,
And there young Rody he must wait until the hour has come,
When a court-martial does arrive for to contrive his doom.

They called upon an arméd band, an arméd band came soon,
To guard the clever tall young youth down to the Bridge of Toome,
And when young Rody he came up the scaffold to ascend,
He looked at east and looked at west to view his loving friends.

And turning round unto the north he cried, "O faithless friend,
'Twas you who proved my overthrow and brought me to this end.
Since 'tis upon Good Friday that I'll executed be,
Convenient to the Bridge of Toome upon a Gallows tree."

They called on Father Devlin, his reverence came with speed,
"Here's one of Christ's own flock," he said, "ye shepherds for to feed."
He gave to him the Heavenly food, that nourishes the soul,
That it may rest eternally while his body is in the mould.

And looking up into the Lord he says, "O Lord receive,
Here is my soul, I do bestow my body unto the grave,
That it may rest in peace and joy without the least surprise,
Till Michael sounds his trumpet loud, and says 'Ye dead arise.'"

TRADITIONAL (19TH CENTURY)

The Wild Colonial Boy

There was a wild colonial boy, Jack Dougan was his name.
He was born and bred in Ireland, in a place called Castlemaine.
He was his father's only son, his mother's pride and joy,
And dearly did his parents love the wild colonial boy.

At the early age of sixteen years he left his native home,
And to Australia's sunny shores he was inclined to roam.
He robbed the rich, he helped the poor, he shot James McEvoy;
A terror to Australia was that wild colonial boy.

One morning on the prairie wide Jack Dougan rode along,
Listening to a mockingbird singing its mocking song.
Out came three mounted troopers—Kelly, Davis, and Fitzroy.
They all went out to capture him, the wild colonial boy.

"Surrender now, Jack Dougan, you see it's three to one,
Surrender in the King's high name for you're a plundering son."
He drew two pistols from his belt and proudly raised them high.
"I'll fight, but not surrender," said the wild colonial boy.

He fired a shot at Kelly which brought him to the ground,
And turning 'round to Davis he received a mortal wound.
A bullet pierced his proud young heart from the pistol of Fitzroy,
And that was how they captured him, the wild colonial boy.

TRADITIONAL (19TH CENTURY)

The Silence of Unlaboured Fields

The silence of unlaboured fields
Lies like a judgement on the air:
A human voice is never heard:
The sighing grass is everywhere—
The sighing grass, the shadowed sky,
The cattle crying wearily!

Where are the lowland people gone?
Where are the sun-dark faces now?
The love that kept the quiet hearth,
The strength that held the speeding plough?
Grasslands and lowing herds are good,
But better human flesh and blood!

JOSEPH CAMPBELL (1879–1944)

The Workman's Friend

When things go wrong and will not come right
Though you do the best you can,
When life looks black as the hour of night,
A PINT OF PLAIN IS YOUR ONLY MAN.

When money's tight and is hard to get
And your horse has also ran,
When all you have is a heap of debt
A PINT OF PLAIN IS YOUR ONLY MAN.

When health is bad and your heart feels strange
And your face is pale and wan,
When doctors say that you need a change
A PINT OF PLAIN IS YOUR ONLY MAN.

When food is scarce and your larder bare
And no rashers grease your pan,
When hunger grows as your meals are rare
A PINT OF PLAIN IS YOUR ONLY MAN.

In time of trouble and lousy strife,
You have still got a darling plan,
You still can turn to a brighter life
A PINT OF PLAIN IS YOUR ONLY MAN.

FLANN O'BRIEN (1911–1966)

To My Son in Americay

[Air: *The Rocks of Knockanure*]

Some years ago in the County Mayo
This story all began,
Before emigration was finally cured
By the first economical plan.
A poor young lad had to leave his home
And travel across the sea,
But he got well paid in the building trade
    On the shores of Americay.

Now he did very well but he sent nothing home
And his mother began to think
That he had run away with a blonde
Or was spending his money on drink,
So she wrote him a letter and folded it up
And sent it on its way
And on the cover she clearly wrote
    "To my son in Americay."

The postman collected to the letter she wrote
And drove in a van to Cork,
Where he put it aboard of a liner at Cobh
That landed it in New York;
And there with the whiskey and the greyhounds too
The mail-bags lay on the quay
And among the rest was a letter addressed
    "To my son in Americay."

Now American postmen I needn't remark
Are rather like me and you,
And when they came to this letter at last
They didn't know what to do.
They consulted all the official lists

But these had nothing to say.
There was no directory would help them to find
    A son in Americay.

So it lay round the office for years and years
And gave all the boys a laugh,
Until it got some use at last
In the training of the staff.
To every new postman that came on the job
It was shown as exhibit A,
As insufficiently addressed
    "To my son in Americay."

The son got older and wiser too
And at last to himself he said
"O how are thing goin' with me mother at home,
And is she alive or dead?"
So he walked round the block to the G.P.O.
And he asked with his cap in his hand,
"Is there any chance you've a letter for me
    From me mother in Ireland?"

"We have indeed sir and here it is,
We've been waiting for you to call,
We knew that some one would come some day
From Cork or Donegal.
From two hundred millions that's livin' now
In the whole of the U.S.A.
For a mother in Ireland at last we've found
    Her son in Americay."

ALF MacLochlainn (1926–)

The Man of the North Countrie

He came from the North, and his words were few,
But his voice was kind and his heart was true;
And I knew by his eyes no guile had he,
So I married the man of the North Countrie.

Oh! Garryowen may be more gay,
Than this quiet street of Ballibay;
And I know the sun shines softly down
On the river that passes my native town.

But there's not—I say it with joy and pride—
Better man than mine in Munster wide;
And Limerick town has no happier hearth
Than mine has been with my man of the North.

I wish that in Munster they only knew
The kind, kind neighbours I came unto:
Small hate or scorn would ever be
Between the South and the North Countrie.

THOMAS D'ARCY McGEE (1825–1868)

The Low-Back'd Car

When first I saw sweet Peggy,
  'Twas on a market day,
A low-back'd car she drove,
  And sat upon a truss of hay;
But when that hay was blooming grass,
  And deck'd with flowers of Spring,
No flow'r was there that could compare
  With the blooming girl I sing!
As she sat in her low-back'd car—
  The man at the turnpike bar
Never ask'd for the toll,
  But just rubb'd his ould poll
And look'd after the low-backed car.

In battle's wild commotion,
  The proud and mighty Mars,
With hostile scythes, demands his tithes
  Of death—in warlike cars;
While Peggy, peaceful goddess,
  Has darts in her bright eye,
That knock men down, in the market town,
  As right and left they fly—
While she sits in her low-back'd car,
  Than battle more dangerous far—
For the doctor's art,
  Cannot cure the heart
That is hit from that low-back'd car.

Sweet Peggy round her car, sir
  Has strings of ducks and geese,
But the scores of hearts she slaughters,
  By far outnumber these;

While she among her poultry sits,
   Just like a turtle dove
Well worth the cage, I do engage,
   Of the blooming god of Love!
While she sits in her low-back'd car,
   The lovers come near and far,
And envy the chicken, that Peggy is pickin'
   While she sits in her low-back'd car.

I'd rather own that car, sir!
   With Peggy by my side,
Than a coach and four, and gold galore
   And a lady for my bride.
For the lady would sit forninst me,
   On a cushion made with taste,
While Peggy would sit beside me,
   With my arm around her waist.
As we drove in the low-back'd car,
   To be married by Father Maher,
Oh, my heart would beat high
   At her glance and her sigh,
Tho' it beat in a low-back'd car.

SAMUEL LOVER (1797–1868)

She Is Far from the Land

She is far from the land where her young hero sleeps,
    And lovers are round her, sighing:
But coldly she turns from their gaze, and weeps,
    For her heart in his grave is lying!

She sings the wild song of her dear native plains,
    Every note which he loved awaking;
Ah! little they think who delight in her strains,
    How the heart of the Minstrel is breaking!

He had lived for his love, for his country he died,
    They were all that to life had entwined him,
Nor soon shall the tears of his country be dried,
    Nor long will his love stay behind him.

Oh! make her a grave, where the sun-beams rest,
    When they promise a glorious morrow;
They'll shine o'er her sleep, like a smile from the West,
    From her own loved Island of sorrow!

THOMAS MOORE (1779–1852)

If I Was a Blackbird

If I was a blackbird I'd whistle and sing
And I'd follow the ship that my true love sails in,
And on the top riggings I'd there build my nest,
And I'd pillow my head on his lily white breast.

I am a young maiden and my story is sad
For once I was courted by a brave sailor lad.
He courted me strongly by night and by day,
But now my dear sailor is gone far away.

He promised to take me to Donnybrook fair,
To buy me red ribbons to tie up my hair.
And when he'd return from the ocean so wide,
He'd take me and make me his own loving bride.

His parents they slight me and will not agree
That I and my sailor boy married should be.
But when he comes home I will greet him with joy
And I'll take to my bosom my dear sailor boy.

TRADITIONAL (18TH CENTURY)

The Croppy Boy

It was early, early, all in the spring
The wee birds whistled and began to sing
They sang so sweet and so joyously
And the song they sang was: Old Ireland Free!

It was early, early last Thursday night
The yeoman cavalry gave me a fright
The yeoman cavalry proved my downfall
I was prisoner taken by Lord Cornwall

It was in his guard-house where I was laid
And in his parlour that I was tried
My sentence passed, and my spirits low
To New Geneva I was forced to go

As I was marching through Wexford Street
The drums and fifes they did play so sweet
The drums and fifes did so sweetly play
While we were marching so far away!

When I was taken by my father's door
My brother William he stood on the floor
My agéd father did grieve full sore
And my tender mother, her hair she tore

When my sister Mary heard the express
She ran downstairs in her morning dress
"Five hundred guineas I would lay down
To set you free in sweet Wexford town"

When I was marching over Wexford Hill
Oh who could blame me for to cry my fill
I looked behind and I looked before
But my tender mother I could see no more

When I was mounted on the gallows high
My agéd father, he was standing by
My agéd father, he did me deny
And the name he gave me was "the Croppy Boy!"

TRADITIONAL (LATE 18TH CENTURY)

PART IV

I LEAVE MY WARM HEART WITH YOU, THOUGH MY BACK I'M FORCED TO TURN

The New Irish Girl

Abroad as I was walking, down by the river side,
A-gazing all around me, an Irish girl I spied.
So red and rosy were her cheeks, and yellow was her hair,
And costly was the robe of gold my Irish girl did wear.

Her shoes of Spanish leather were all spangled round with dew,
She wrung her hands, and tore her hair, crying, "Ah, what can I do?
I'm going home, I'm going home, I'll quit this counterie,
Why will you go a-roving and slight your dear Polly?"

The last time that I saw my love, he seemed to be in pain,
With chilling grief and anguish, his heart was broke in twain;
There's many a man that's worse than me, so why should I complain?
O! Love it is a killing thing, did you ever feel the pain?

I wish my love was a red, red rose, that in the garden grew,
And I to be the gardener, to her I would prove true;
There's not a month throughout the year, but my love I would renew,
With lilies I would garnish her, Sweet William, thyme, and rue.

I wisht I was a butterfly, I'd fly to my love's breast,
I wisht I was a linnet and I'd sing my love to rest,
I wisht I was a blue cuckoo, I'd sing till morning clear,
I'd sing and sing for you, my girl, I once did love so dear.

TRADITIONAL (LATE 18TH CENTURY)

Kilcash

What shall we do for timber?
    The last of the woods is down.
Kilcash and the house of its glory
    And the bell of the house are gone,
The spot where that lady waited
    Who shamed all women for grace
When earls came sailing to greet her
    And Mass was said in the place.

My grief and my affliction
    Your gates are taken away,
Your avenue needs attention,
    Goats in the garden stray.
The courtyard's filled with water
    And the great earls where are they?
The earls, the lady, the people
    Beaten into the clay.

No sound of duck or geese there,
    Hawk's cry or eagle's call,
No humming of the bees there
    That brought honey and wax for all,
Nor even the sound of the birds there
    When the sun goes down in the west,
No cuckoo on top of the boughs there,
    Singing the world to rest.

There's mist there tumbling from branches,
    Unstirred by night and by day,
And darkness falling from heaven,
    For our fortune has ebbed away,

There's no holly nor hazel nor ash there,
    The pasture's rock and stone,
The crown of the forest has withered,
    And the last of its game is gone.

I beseech of Mary and Jesus
    That the great come home again
With long dances danced in the garden,
    Fiddle music and mirth among men,
That Kilcash the home of our fathers
    Be lifted on high again,
And from that to the deluge of waters
    In bounty and peace remain.

TRADITIONAL (18TH CENTURY)
translated from the Irish by Frank O'Connor

The Outlaw of Loch Lene

O many a day have I made good ale in the glen,
That came not of stream or malt—like the brewing of men.
My bed was the ground; my roof, the greenwood above,
And the wealth that I sought, one far kind glance from my love.

Alas! on that night when the horses I drove from the field,
That I was not near from terror my angel to shield.
She stretched forth her arms; her mantle she flung to the wind,
And swam o'er Loch Lene, her outlawed lover to find.

O would that a freezing sleet-winged tempest did sweep,
And I and my love were alone, far off on the deep;
I'd ask not a ship, or a bark, or a pinnace, to save—
With her hand round my waist, I'd fear not the wind or the wave.

'Tis down by the lake where the wild-tree fringes its sides,
The maid of my heart, my fair one of Heaven resides;—
I think, as at eve she wanders its mazes among,
The birds go to sleep by the sweet wild twist of her song.

TRADITIONAL
translated from the Irish by Jeremiah Joseph Callanan

Moorloch Mary

Like swords of battle the scythes were plying,
The corn lay low in a yellow rout,
When down the stubble, dew-wet and glinting,
A golden shaft of the sun came out:
It was Moorloch Mary, the slender blossom,
Who smiled on me in the misty morn,
And since that hour I am lost with grieving,
Through sleepless nights, and through days forlorn.

Oh Moorloch lies in a world of heather
Where Mary's little brown feet go bare,
And many a shadowy peak divides us,
Yet I will journey to find her there:
I will climb the mountains and swim the rivers,
I will travel the crests of the heath, wind-blown;
Her face in my heart like a star I carry,
And it shall guide me unto my own.

When I come at last to my Moorloch Mary,
I will take her little brown hands in mine,
And kiss her lips where the rowans tarry,
And kiss her hair where the sun-rays shine;
And whisper—"Astórin, my heart was haunted
By wistful eyes of the sweetest grey,
That drew it over the hills of Derry—
O Moorloch Mary, bid the wanderer stay."

ETHNA CARBERY (1866–1902)

A Glass of Beer

The lanky hank of a she in the inn over there
Nearly killed me for asking the loan of a glass of beer;
May the devil grip the whey-faced slut by the hair,
And beat bad manners out of her skin for a year.

That parboiled imp, with the toughest jaw you will see
On virtue's path, and a voice that would rasp the dead,
Came roaring and raging the minute she looked at me,
And threw me out of the house on the back of my head!

If I asked her master he'd give me a cask a day;
But she, with the beer at hand, not a gill would arrange!
May she marry a ghost and bear him a kitten, and may
The High King of Glory permit her to get the mange.

JAMES STEPHENS (1882–1950)

The Blind Traveller

Tyrone twice over I've walked with the tinker that's blind
County Mayo and enough of the county Meath
I'm always hungry and many and many's the time
I've walked hard roads without any shoes to my feet

He went and he got himself a few yards of hempen cord
One end in his hand the other around me he'd wind
Lest any odd stroller that's going the road half-jarred
Got a notion of hugging the wife of a man that's blind

It's a pity I wasn't already left dead in my grave
Before I got bound to him for the rest of my life
It was a sorrowful day when marriage made me a slave
Like a beast at the end of a tether a blind man's wife

Better years in the ocean fighting the stormy waves
Than always to hear the harsh word of the man without eyes
He can't even see a candle in front of his face
Never mind the full moon or the shooting stars crossing the skies

It's the pain of the world that I'm tied to a man without sight
When another man spoke mad jealous he was at the sound
Of my chatting a bit just the way that any girl might
I'll cut through the rope let him fall in a bog-hole and drown.

TRADITIONAL
translated from the Irish by Alf MacLochlainn

Me an' Me Da

I'm livin' in Drumlister,
An' I'm gettin very oul'
I have to wear an Indian bag
To save me from the coul'.
The deil a man in this townlan'
Wos claner raired nor me,
But I'm livin' in Drumlister
In clabber to the knee.

Me da lived up in Carmin,
An' kep' a sarvint boy;
His second wife was very sharp,
He birried her with joy:
Now she was thin, her name was Flynn,
She come from Cullentra,
An' if me shirt's a clatty shirt
The man to blame's me da.

Consarnin' weemin, sure it was
A constant word of his,
"Keep far away from them that's thin,
Their temper's aisy riz."
Well, I knowed two I thought wud do,
But still I had me fears,
So I kiffled back an' forrit
Between the two, for years.

Wee Margit had no fortune
But two rosy cheeks wud plaze;
The farm of lan' wos Bridget's,
But she tuk the pock disayse:
An' Margit she wos very wee,

An' Bridget she was stout
But her face wos like a gaol dure
With the bowlts pulled out.

I'll tell no lie on Margit,
She thought the worl' of me;
I'll tell the truth, me heart wud lep
The sight of her to see
But I was slow, ye surely know,
The raison of it now,
If I left her home from Carmin
Me da wud rise a row.

So I swithered back an' forrit
Till Margit got a man;
A fella come from Mullaslin
An' left me jist the wan.
I mind the day she went away,
I hid wan strucken hour,
An' cursed the wasp from Cullentra
That made me da so sour.

But cryin' cures no trouble,
To Bridget I went back,
An' faced her for it that night week
Beside her own turf-stack.
I axed her there, an' spoke her fair,
The handy wife she'd make me.
I talked about the lan' that joined
—Begob, she wudn't take me!

So I'm livin' in Drumlister,
An' I'm gettin' very oul'.
I creep to Carmin wanst a month
To thry an' make me sowl:

The deil a man in this townlan'
Wos claner raired nor me,
An' I'm dyin' in Drumlister
In clabber to the knee.

THE REVEREND WILLIAM MARSHALL (1888–1959)

The Galbally Farmer

One evening of late as I happened to stray
To the county Tipp'rary I straight took my way
To dig the potatoes and work by the day
I hired with a Galbally farmer.
I asked him how far we were bound for to go
The night being dark and the north wind did blow
I was hungry and tired and my spirits were low
For I got neither whiskey nor cordial.

This miserable miser, he mounted his steed
To the Galbally Mountains he hastened with speed
And surely I thought that my poor heart would bleed
As I tried to keep up with his travel.
When we came to his cottage, I entered it first
It seemed like a kennel or a ruined old church
Says I to myself "I am left in the lurch
In the house of old Darby O'Leary!"

I well recollect it was Michaelmas Night
To a hearty good supper he did me invite
A cup of sour milk that was more green than white
'Twould give you the trotting disorder.
The wet old potatoes would poison the cat
And the barn where my bed was was swarming with rats
'Twas little I thought it would e'er be my lot
To lie in that hole until mornings.

By what he had said to me I understood
My bed in the barn it was not very good
The blanket was made at the time of the flood
The quilt and the sheets in proportion.
'Twas on this old miser I looked with a frown

When the straw was brought out for to make my shake-down
And I wished that I never saw Galbally Town
Or the sky over Darby O'Leary!

I've worked in Kilconnel, I've worked in Kilmore
I've worked in Knockainy and Shanballymore
In Pallas-A-Nicrer and Sollohodmore
With decent respectable farmers.
I worked in Tipperary, the Rag, and Rosegreen
At the Mount of Kilfeakle, the Bridge of Aleen
But such woeful starvation I have never yet seen
Than I got from old Darby O'Leary!

DIARMUID O'RIAIN (1777–1885)

An Elegy on the Death of a Mad Dog

Good people, all, of every sort,
Give ear unto my song;
And if you find it wond'rous short,
It cannot hold you long.

In Islington there was a man,
Of whom the world might say,
That still a godly race he ran,
Whene'er he went to pray.

A kind and gentle heart he had,
To comfort friends and foes;
The naked every day he clad,
When he put on his clothes.

And in that town a dog was found,
As many dogs there be,
Both mongrel, puppy, whelp, and hound,
And curs of low degree.

This dog and man at first were friends;
But when a pique began,
The dog, to gain some private ends,
Went mad and bit the man.

Around from all the neighbouring streets
The wondering neighbours ran,
And swore the dog had lost his wits,
To bite so good a man.

The wound it seemed both sore and sad
To every Christian eye;
And while they swore the dog was mad,
They swore the man would die.

But soon a wonder came to light,
That showed the rogues they lied:
The man recovered of the bite,
The dog it was that died.

Oliver Goldsmith (1728–1774)

The Ould Orange Flute

In the County Tyrone, near the town of Dungannon,
Where many a ruction myself had a han' in,
Bob Williamson lived, a weaver by trade,
And all of us thought him a stout Orange blade.
On the Twelfth of July, as it yearly did come,
Bob played on the flute to the sound of the drum—
You may talk of your harp, your piano, or lute,
But nothing could sound like the ould Orange flute.

But this treacherous scoundrel he took us all in,
For he married a Papish called Bridget McGinn;
Turned Papish himself, and forsook the old cause
That gave us our freedom, religion and laws.
Now, the boys in the townland made some noise upon it,
And Bob had to fly to the province of Connacht,
He flew with his wife and fixings to boot,
And along with the others the ould Orange flute.

At chapel on Sundays to atone for his past deeds,
He'd say Paters and Aves, and count his brown beads,
Till, after some time, at the priest's own desire,
He went with that ould flute to play in the choir,
He went with that ould flute to play in the loft,
But the instrument shivered and sighed and then coughed.
When he blew it and fingered it, it made a strange noise,
For the flute would play only the "Protestant Boys."

Bob jumped up and started and got in a flutter,
And he put the ould flute in the bless'd holy water;
He thought that it might now make some other sound,
When he blew it again it played, "Croppies, Lie Down!"
And all he did whistle, and finger, and blow,

To play Papish music he found it "no go."
"Kick the Pope," "The Boyne Water," and such like 'twould sound,
But one Papish squeak in it couldn't be found.

At a council of priests that was held the next,
They decided to banish the ould flute away;
As they couldn't knock heresy out of its head,
They bought Bob another to play in its stead.
So the ould flute was doomed and its fate was pathetic,
It was fastened and burned at the stake as heretic.
While the flames roared round it, they heard a strange noise,
The ould flute was still playing the "Protestant Boys."

TRADITIONAL

The Winding Banks of Erne

Adieu to Ballyshannon! where I was bred and born;
Go where I may, I'll think of you, as sure as night and morn,
The kindly spot, the friendly town, where everyone is known,
And not a face in all the place but partly seems my own;
There's not a house or window, there's not a field or hill,
But, east or west, in foreign lands, I'll recollect them still.
I leave my warm heart with you, though my back I'm forced to turn—
So adieu to Ballyshannon, and the winding banks of Erne!

No more on pleasant evenings we'll saunter down the Mall,
When the trout is rising to the fly, the salmon to the fall.
The boat comes straining on her net, and heavily she creeps,
Cast off, cast off!—she feels the oars, and to her berth she sweeps;
Now fore and aft keep hauling, and gathering up the clue,
Till a silver wave of salmon rolls in among the crew.
Then they may sit, with pipes a-lit, and many a joke and "yarn";
Adieu to Ballyshannon, and the winding banks of Erne!

The music of the waterfall, the mirror of the tide,
When all the green-hill'd harbour is full from side to side—
From Portnasun to Bulliebawns, and round the Abbey Bay,
From rocky Inis Saimer to Coolnargit sandhills grey;
While far upon the southern line, to guard it like a wall,
The Leitrim mountains, clothed in blue, gaze calmly over all,
And watch the ship sail up or down, the red flag at her stern;
Adieu to these, adieu to all the winding banks of Erne!

Farewell to you, Kildoney lads, and them that pull an oar,
A lug-sail set, or haul a net, from the point of Mullaghmore;
From Killybegs to bold Slieve-League, that ocean-mountain steep,
Six hundred yards in air aloft, six hundred in the deep;
From Dooran to the Fairy Bridge, and round by Tullan Strand,

Level and long, and white with waves, where gull and curlew stand-
Head out to sea, when on your lee the breakers you discern!—
Adieu to all the billowy coast, and the winding banks of Erne!

Farewell Coolmore, —Bundoran! and your summer crowds that run
From inland homes to see with joy th' Atlantic-setting sun;
To breathe the buoyant salted air, and sport among the waves;
To gather shells on sandy beach, and tempt the gloomy caves;
To watch the flowing, ebbing tide, the boats, the crabs, the fish;
Young men and maids to meet and smile, and form a tender wish;
The sick and old in search of health, for all things have their turn—
And I must quit my native shore, and the winding banks of Erne!

Farewell to every white cascade from the Harbour to Belleek,
And every pool where fins may rest, and ivy-shaded creek;
The sloping fields, the lofty rocks, where ash and holly grow,
The one split yew-tree gazing on the curving flood below;
The Lough, that winds through islands under Turaw Mountain green;
And Castle Caldwell's stretching woods, with tranquil bays between;
And Breesie Hill, and many a pond among the heath and fern,—
For I must say adieu—adieu to the winding banks of Erne!

The thrush will call through Camlin groves the live-long summer day;
The waters run by mossy cliff, and bank with wild flowers gay;
The girls will bring their work and sing beneath a twisted thorn,
Or stray with sweethearts down the path among the growing corn;
Along the river side they go, where I have often been,—
O, never shall I see again the days that I have seen!
A thousand chances are to one I never may return,—
Adieu to Ballyshannon, and the winding banks of Erne!

Adieu to evening dances, where merry neighbours meet,
And the fiddle says to boys and girls, "Get up and shake your feet!"
To "shanachus" and wise old talk of Erin's days gone by,—
Who trench'd the rath on such a hill, and where the bones may lie

Of saint, or king, or warrior chief; with tales of fairy power,
And tender ditties sweetly sung to pass the twilight hour.
The mournful song of exile is now for me to learn—
Adieu, my dear companions on the winding banks of Erne!

Now measure from the Commons down to each end of the Purt,
Round the Abbey, Moy and Knather—I wish no one any hurt;
The Main Street, Back Street, College Lane, the Mall and Portnasun,
If any foes of mine are there, I pardon every one.
I hope that man and womankind will do the same by me;
For my heart is sore and heavy at voyaging the sea.
My loving friends I'll bear in mind, and often fondly turn
To think of Ballyshannon and the winding banks of Erne!

If ever I'm a money'd man, I mean, please God, to cast
My golden anchor in the place where youthful years were past;
Though heads that now are black and brown must meanwhile gather
    grey,
New faces rise by every hearth, and old ones drop away—
Yet dearer still that Irish hill than all the world beside;
It's home, sweet home, where'er I roam, through lands and waters wide;
And if the Lord allows me, I surely will return
To my native Ballyshannon, and the winding banks of Erne!

WILLIAM ALLINGHAM (1824–1889)

Love Is Pleasing

I wish, I wish, I wish in vain
I wish I were a maid again
But a maid again I can never be
Until apples grow on an ivy tree

For love is pleasing and love is teasing
And love is a treasure when first it's new
But as love grows older then love grows colder
And it fades away like the morning dew

There is an alehouse in the town
And there my love he sits him down
He takes a strange girl on his knee
And he tells her things that he once told me

For love and porter make a young girl older
And love and whiskey make her old and grey
And what cannot be cured, love, must be endured, love
And now I am bound for Amerikay

TRADITIONAL

Thomas MacDonagh

He shall not hear the bittern cry
In the wild sky, where he is lain,
Nor voices of the sweeter birds
Above the wailing of the rain.

Nor shall he know when loud March blows
Thro' slanting snows her fanfare shrill,
Blowing to flame the golden cup
Of many an upset daffodil.

But when the Dark Cow leaves the moor,
And pastures poor with greedy weeds,
Perhaps he'll hear her low at morn
Lifting her horn in pleasant meads.

FRANCIS LEDWIDGE (1887–1917)

The Convict of Clonmel

How hard is my fortune
And vain my repining!
The strong rope of Fate
For this young neck is twining.
My strength is departed,
My cheeks sunk and sallow,
While I languish in chains
In the gaol of Clonmala.

No boy of the village
Was ever yet milder,
I'd play with a child
And my sport would be wilder.
I'd dance without tiring
From morning 'till even,
And the goal-ball I'd strike
To the light'ning of Heaven.

At my bed foot decaying,
My hurl-bat is lying,
Through the boys of the village
My goal-ball is flying.
My horse 'mong the neighbours,
Neglected may fallow,
While I pine in my chains
In the gaol of Clonmala.

Next Sunday the patron
At home will be keeping,
And the young, active hurlers
The field will be sweeping.
With the dance of fair maidens

The evening they'll hallow,
While this heart, once so warm
Will be cold in Clonmala.

TRADITIONAL (18TH CENTURY)
translated from the Irish by Jeremiah Joseph Callanan

PART V

THEN FURTHER GOING
MY WILD OATS SOWING
TO NEW YORK CITY
I CROSSED THE SEA

The Lambs on the Green Hills

The lambs on the green hills stood gazing on me,
And many strawberries grew round the salt sea,
And many strawberries grew round the salt sea,
And many a ship sailed the ocean.

And bride and bride's party to church they did go,
The bride she rode foremost, she bears the best show,
But I followed after with my heart full of woe,
To see my love wed to another.

The first place I saw her 'twas in the church stand,
Gold rings on her finger and her love by the hand,
Says I, "My wee lassie, I will be the man
Although you are wed to another."

The next place I saw her was on the way home,
I ran on before her, not knowing where to roam,
Says I, "My wee lassie, I'll be by your side
Although you are wed to another."

The next place I saw her 'twas laid in bride's bed,
I jumped in beside her and did kiss the bride;
"Stop, stop," said the groomsman, "till I speak a word,
Will you venture your life on the point of my sword?
For courting so slowly you've lost this fair maid,
So begone, for you'll never enjoy her."

Oh, make my grave then both large, wide and deep,
And sprinkle it over with flowers so sweet,
And lay me down in it to take my last sleep,
For that's the best way to forget her.

TRADITIONAL

A White Rose

The red rose whispers of passion,
   And the white rose breathes of love;
Oh, the red rose is a falcon,
   And the white rose is a dove.

But I send you a cream-white rosebud
   With a flush on its petal tips;
For the love that is purest and sweetest
   Has a kiss of desire on the lips.

JOHN BOYLE O'REILLY (1844–1890)

My Love Is Like the Sun

The winter is past,
And the summer's come at last
And the blackbirds sing in every tree;
The hearts of these are glad
But my poor heart is sad,
Since my true love is absent from me.

The rose upon the briar
By the water running clear
Gives joy to the linnet and the bee;
Their little hearts are blest
But mine is not at rest,
While my true love is absent from me.

A livery I'll wear
And I'll comb out my hair,
And in velvet so green I'll appear,
And straight I will repair
To the Curragh of Kildare
For it's there I'll find tidings of my dear.

I'll wear a cap of black
With a frill around my neck,
Gold rings on my fingers I'll wear:
All this I'll undertake
For my true lover's sake,
He resides at the Curragh of Kildare.

I would not think it strange
Thus the world for to range,
If I only get tidings of my dear;
But here in Cupid's chain

If I'm bound to remain,
I would spend my whole life in despair.

My love is like the sun
That in the firmament does run,
And always proves constant and true;
But he is like the moon
That wanders up and down,
And every month is new.

All ye that are in love
And cannot it remove,
I pity the pains you endure;
For experience lets me know
That your hearts are full of woe,
And a woe that no mortal can cure.

TRADITIONAL

The Spanish Man

There were lovely ladies along the Claddagh
All taking the air by each garden tree,
All taking air in the quiet evening,
And none so lovely as my lady.

Then I stepped beside her most entertaining,
Making fine talk on the rounded sea,
"But ah," she said, "you I cannot marry,
For a bold Spanish man said bravely to me:

"'Oh be my lady, and in Limerick laces
Your delicate ways shall airily pass,
With quiet feet in your blue pampooties
And guinea hens on the daisied grass.'"

F. R. HIGGINS (1896–1941)

Oh! Breathe Not His Name

Oh! breathe not his name, let it sleep in the shade
Where, cold and unhonoured, his relics are laid:
Sad, silent, and dark, be the tears that we shed,
As the night-dew that falls on the grass o'er his head.

But the night-dew that falls, though in silence it weeps,
Shall brighten with verdure the grave where he sleeps;
And the tear that we shed, though in secret it rolls,
Shall long keep his memory green in our souls.

THOMAS MOORE (1779–1852)

Les Silhouettes

The sea is flecked with bars of grey,
    The dull dead wind is out of tune,
And like a withered leaf the moon
    Is blown across the stormy bay.

Etched clear upon the pallid sand
    Lies the black boat: a sailor boy
Clambers aboard in careless joy
    With laughing face and gleaming hand.

And overhead the curlews cry,
    Where through the dusky upland grass
The young brown-throated reapers pass,
    Like silhouettes against the sky.

OSCAR WILDE (1854–1900)

Here's to the Maiden

Here's to the maiden of bashful fifteen,
    Here's to the widow of fifty;
Here's to the flaunting extravagant quean,
    And here's to the housewife that's thrifty!

    Let the toast pass,
    Drink to the lass,
I'll warrant she'll prove an excuse for the glass.

Here's to the charmer whose dimples we prize;
    Now to the maid who has none, sir:
Here's to the girl with a pair of blue eyes,
    And here's to the nymph with but one, sir!

    Let the toast pass,
    Drink to the lass,
I'll warrant she'll prove an excuse for the glass.

Here's to the maid with a bosom of snow;
    Now to her that's as brown as a berry:
Here's to the wife with her face full of woe,
    And now to the damsel that's merry!

    Let the toast pass,
    Drink to the lass,
I'll warrant she'll prove an excuse for the glass.

For let 'em be clumsy, or let 'em be slim,
    Young or ancient, I care not a feather;
So fill a pint bumper quite up to the brim,
    And let us e'en toast them together.

Let the toast pass,
Drink to the lass,
I'll warrant she'll prove an excuse for the glass.

RICHARD BRINSLEY SHERIDAN (1751–1816)

The Spanish Lady

As I walked down through Dublin City
At the hour of twelve in the night,
Who should I spy but a Spanish Lady,
Washing her feet by candlelight?
First she dipped them, and then she dried them,
Over a fire of ambery coal.
Never in all my life did I see
A maid so neat about the sole.

I stopped to peep, but the Watchman passed,
And says: Young fellow, the night is late.
Get home to bed, or I'll wrastle you
At a double trot through the Bridewell gate!
So I waved a kiss to the Spanish Lady,
Hot as the fire of cramesy coal.
I've seen dark maids, though never one
So white and neat about the sole.

O, she's too rich for a Poddle swaddy,
With her tortoise comb and mantle fine.
A Hellfire buck would fit her better,
Drinking brandy and claret wine.
I'm just a decent College sizar,
Poor as a sod of smouldery coal;
And how would I dress the Spanish Lady,
And she so neat about the sole?

O, she'd make a mott for the Provost Marshal,
Or a wife for the Mayor on his coach so high,
Or a queen of Andalusia,
Kicking her heel in the Cardinal's eye.
I'm blue as cockles, brown as herrings

Over a grid of glimmery coal,
And all because of the Spanish Lady,
So mortial neat about the sole.

I wandered north, and I wandered south,
By Golden Lane and Patrick's Close,
The Coombe, Smithfield and Stoneybatter,
Back to Napper Tandy's house.
Old age has laid its hand upon me,
Cold as a fire of ashy coal.—
And where is the lovely Spanish Lady,
That maid so neat about the sole?

JOSEPH CAMPBELL (1879–1944)

Whiskey in Me Tay

Come all ye bold teetotallers and list' to me a while,
And if you close attention pay I'll cause you to smile;
No story of Grecian queen, nor tale of Trojan say
But a tale of woe that happened so with whiskey in me tay.

I was a bold teetotaller for three long years and more,
The neighbours all respected me and decent clothes I wore,
My family were fond of me till one unlucky day
Just like a child I was beguiled with whiskey in me tay.

I only took the smallest sup when up the ructions rose,
I saw that I was put upon and slaughtered friends and foes,
A Polisman surrounded me and hauled me up next day,
The charge was read and duly pled, 'twas whiskey in me tay.

From Carrickmacross to Crossmaglen the polisman did vow
There are more rogues than honest men as any will allow,
It isn't rogues or honest men the Justice then did say,
We deal with now, but a drunken row from whiskey in his tay.

This man he was a sober man for three long years or more
The neighbours all respected him and decent clothes he wore,
The story is an ancient one the justice did say,
He'll pay up bail or go to gaol for whiskey in his tay.

So all bold teetotalers if sober you would be
Be careful of your company and mind what happened to me,
It wasn't the lads from Shercock or the boys from Ballybay,
But the dealing men from Crossmaglen put whiskey in me tay.

TRADITIONAL (19TH CENTURY)

Epigrams

I. May we never taste of death nor quit this vale of tears
Until we see the Englishry go begging down the years,
Packs on their backs to earn a penny pay,
In little leaking boots, as we did in our day.

II. Time has o'erthrown, the wind has blown away
Alastair, Caesar, such great names as they—
See Troy and Tara where in grass they lie—
Even the very English might yet die!

TRADITIONAL (17TH CENTURY)
translated from the Irish by Maire MacEntee

Sweet Omagh Town

Ah! from proud Dungannon to Ballyshannon
And from Cullyhanna to Old Ardboe
I've roused and rambled, caroused and gambled
Where songs did thunder and whiskey flow.
It's light and airy I've tramped through Derry
And to Portaferry in the County Down
But with all my raking and undertaking
My heart was aching for sweet Omagh Town.

When life grew weary, aye, and I grew dreary
I set sail for England from Derry Quay
And when I landed, sure 'twas fate commanded
That I to London should make my way
Where many a gay night from dark to daylight
I spent with people of high renown
But with all their splendour and heaps to spend sure
My heart was empty for sweet Omagh Town.

Then further going my wild oats sowing
To New York City I crossed the sea
Where congregations of rich relations
Stood on the harbour to welcome me
In grand apparel like Duke or Earl
They tried to raise me with sword and crown
But with all their glamour and uproarious manner
My lips would stammer—sweet Omagh Town.

And when life is over and I shall hover
Above the gates where Saint Peter stands
And he shall call me for to install me
Among the saints in those golden lands
And I shall answer "I'm sure 'tis grand sir

For to play the harp and to wear the crown
But I, being humble, sure I'll never grumble
If Heaven's as charming as sweet Omagh Town."

TRADITIONAL (19TH CENTURY)

The Old Bog Road

My feet are here on Broadway
This blessed harvest morn,
But oh! the ache that's in my heart
For the spot where I was born.
My weary hands are blistered
Through work in cold and heat!
And oh! to swing a scythe once more
Through a field of Irish wheat.
Had I the chance to wander back,
Or own a king's abode.
I'd sooner see the hawthorn tree
By the Old Bog Road.

When I was young and restless
My mind was ill at ease,
Through dreaming of America,
And the gold beyond the seas.
Oh, sorrow take their money,
'Tis hard to find the same,
And what's the world to any man
If no one speaks his name.
I've had my day and here I am
A-building bricks per load,
A long three thousand miles away
From the Old Bog Road.

My mother died last springtime,
When Erin's fields were green.
The neighbours said her waking
Was the finest ever seen.
There were snowdrops and primroses
Piled high above her bed,

And Ferns Church was crowded
When her funeral Mass was read.
And here was I on Broadway
A-building bricks per load
When they carried out her coffin
Down the Old Bog Road.

There was a decent girl at home
Who used to walk with me.
Her eyes were soft and sorrowful
Like moonlight o'er the sea.
Her name was Mary Dwyer,
But that was long ago.
The ways of God are wiser
Than the things that man might know.
She died the day I left her,
A-building bricks per load,
I'd best forget the days I've spent
On the Old Bog Road.

Ah! Life's a weary puzzle,
Past finding out by man,
I'll take the day for what it's worth
And do the best I can.
Since no one cares a rush for me
What need is there to moan,
I'll go my way and draw my pay
And smoke my pipe alone.
Each human heart must bear its grief
Though bitter be the 'bode
So God be with you, Ireland,
And the Old Bog Road.

TERESA BRAYTON (1868–1943)

PART VI

SO FILL TO ME
THE PARTING GLASS

She Moved through the Fair

My young love said to me, "My brothers won't mind,
And my parents won't slight you for your lack of kind."
Then she stepped away from me, and this she did say
"It will not be long, love, till our wedding day."

She stepped away from me and she moved through the fair,
And fondly I watched her go here and go there,
Then she went her way homeward with one star awake,
As the swan in the evening moves over the lake.

The people were saying no two were ere wed
But one had a sorrow that never was said,
And I smiled as she passed with her goods and her gear,
And that was the last that I saw of my dear.

I dreamt it last night that my young love came in,
So softly she entered, her feet made no din;
She came close beside me, and this she did say
"It will not be long, love, till our wedding day."

PADRAIC COLUM (1881–1972)

The Three Jolly Pigeons

Let schoolmasters puzzle their brain
    With grammar, and nonsense, and learning;
Good liquor, I stoutly maintain,
    Gives *genus* a better discerning.
Let them brag of their heathenish gods,
    Their Lethes, their Styxes, and Stygians,
Their *quis*, and their *quæs*, and their *quods*,
    They're all but a parcel of Pigeons.
                    Toroddle, toroddle, toroll.

When Methodist preachers come down,
    A-preaching that drinking is sinful,
I'll wager the rascals a crown,
    They always preach best with a skinfull.
But when you come down with your pence,
    For a slice of their scurvy religion,
I'll leave it to all men of sense,
    But you, my good friend, are the Pigeon.
                    Toroddle, toroddle, toroll.

Then come, put the jorum about,
    And let us be merry and clever,
Our hearts and our liquors are stout,
    Here's the Three Jolly Pigeons for ever.
Let some cry up woodcock or hare,
    Your bustards, your ducks, and your widgeons;
But of all the gay birds in the air,
    Here's health to the Three Jolly Pigeons.
                    Toroddle, toroddle, toroll.

OLIVER GOLDSMITH (1728–1774)

A Pair of Brown Eyes

One summer evening drunk to hell
I sat there nearly lifeless
An old man in the corner sang
Where the water lilies grow
And on the jukebox Johnny sang
About a thing called love
And it's how are you kid and
    what's your name
And how would you bloody know

In blood and death 'neath a
    screaming sky
I lay down on the ground
And the arms and legs of other men
Were scattered all around
Some cursed some prayed,
    some prayed then cursed
Then prayed and bled some more
And the only thing that I could see
Was a pair of brown eyes that was
    looking at me
But when we got back
    labelled parts one to three
There was no pair of brown eyes
    waiting for me.

And a rovin' a rovin' a rovin' I'll go
For a pair of brown eyes

I looked at him he looked at me
    all I could do was hate him

While Ray and Philomena sang
    of my elusive dreams
I saw the streams the rolling hills
Where his brown eyes were waiting
And I thought about
    a pair of brown eyes
That waited once for me

So drunk to hell I left the place
Sometimes crawling sometimes walking
A hungry sound
    came across the breeze
So, I gave the walls a talking
And I heard the sounds of long ago
    from the old canal
And the birds were whistling
    in the trees
Where the wind was gently laughing

And a rovin' a rovin' a rovin' I'll go
For a pair of brown eyes

SHANE MacGOWAN (1957–)

Ringsend

(After reading Tolstoi)

I will live in Ringsend
With a red-headed whore,
And the fan-light gone in
Where it lights the hall-door;
And listen each night
For her querulous shout,
As at last she streels in
And the pubs empty out.
To soothe that wild breast
With my old-fangled songs,
Till she feels it redressed
From inordinate wrongs,
Imagined, outrageous,
Preposterous wrongs,
Till peace at last comes,
Shall be all I will do,
Where the little lamp blooms
Like a rose in the stew;
And up the back-garden
The sound comes to me
Of the lapsing, unsoilable,
Whispering sea.

OLIVER ST. JOHN GOGARTY (1878–1957)

The Night Before Larry Was Stretched

The night before Larry was stretched,
The boys they all paid him a visit;
A bait in their sacks, too, they fetched;
They sweated their duds till they riz it:
For Larry was ever the lad,
When a boy was condemned to the squeezer,
Would fence all the duds that he had
To help a poor friend to a sneezer,
And warm his gob 'fore he died.

The boys they came crowding in fast,
They drew all their stools round about him,
Six glims round his trap-case were placed,
He couldn't be well waked without 'em.
When one of us asked could he die
Without having truly repented?
Says Larry, "That's all in my eye;
And first by the clargy invented,
To get a fat bit for themselves."

"I'm sorry, dear Larry," says I,
"To see you in this situation;
And blister my limbs if I lie,
I'd as lieve it had been my own station."
"Ochone! it's all over," says he,
"For the neck-cloth I'll be forced to put on,
And by this time tomorrow you'll see
Your poor Larry as dead as a mutton,
Because, why, his courage was good.

"And I'll be cut up like a pie,
And my nob from my body be parted."

"You're in the wrong box, then," says I,
"For blast me if they're so hardhearted;
A chalk on the back of your neck
Is all that Jack Ketch dares to give you;
Then mind not such trifles a feck,
For why should the likes of them grieve you?
And now, boys, come tip us the deck."

The cards being called for, they played,
Till Larry found one of them cheated;
A dart at his napper he made
(The boy being easily heated);
"Oh, by the hokey, you thief,
I'll scuttle your nob with my daddle!
You cheat me because I'm in grief,
But soon I'll demolish your noddle,
And leave you your claret to drink."

Then the clergy came in with his book,
He spoke him so smooth and so civil;
Larry tipped him a Kilmainham look,
And pitched his big wig to the devil;
Then sighing, he threw back his head,
To get a sweet drop of the bottle,
And pitiful sighing, he said:
"Oh, the hemp will be soon round my throttle,
And choke my poor windpipe to death.

"Though sure it's the best way to die,
Oh, the devil a better a-living!
For, sure when the gallows is high
Your journey is shorter to heaven:
But what harasses Larry the most,
And makes his poor soul melancholy,
Is to think on the time when his ghost

Will come in a sheet to sweet Molly—
Oh, sure it will kill her alive!"

So moving these last words he spoke,
We all vented our tears in a shower;
For my part, I thought my heart broke,
To see him cut down like a flower.
On his travels we watched him next day,
Oh, the throttler! I thought I could kill him;
But Larry not one word did say,
Nor changed till he came to King William—
Then, musha! his colour grew white.

When he came to the nubbling chit,
He was tucked up so neat and so pretty,
The rumbler jogged off from his feet,
And he died with his feet to the city;
He kicked, too—but that was all pride,
But soon you might see 'twas all over;
Soon after the noose was untied.
And at darky we waked him in clover,
And sent him to take a ground sweat.

TRADITIONAL (18TH CENTURY)

Song of the Ghost

When all were dreaming
  But Pastheen Power,
A light came streaming
  Beneath her bower:
A heavy foot
  At her door delayed,
A heavy hand
  On the latch was laid.

"Now who dare venture,
  At this dark hour,
Unbid to enter
  My maiden bower?"
"Dear Pastheen, open
  The door to me,
And your true lover
  You'll surely see."

"My own true lover,
  So tall and brave,
Lives exiled over
  The angry wave."
"Your true loves body
  Lies on the bier,
His faithful spirit
  Is with you here."

"His look was cheerful,
  His voice was gay;
Your speech is fearful,
  Your face is grey;

And sad and sunken
　Your eye of blue,
But Patrick, Patrick,
　Alas! 'tis you!"

Ere dawn was breaking
　She heard below
The two cocks shaking
　Their wings to crow.
"Oh, hush you, hush you,
　Both red and grey,
Or you will hurry
　My love away.

"Oh, hush your crowing,
　Both grey and red,
Or he'll be going
　To join the dead;
Or, cease from calling
　His ghost to the mould,
And I'll come crowning
　Your combs with gold."

When all were dreaming
　But Pastheen Power,
A light went streaming
　From out her bower;
And on the morrow,
　When they awoke,
They knew that sorrow
　Her heart had broke.

Alfred Percival Graves (1846–1931)

The Ballad of William Bloat

In a mean abode on the Shankill Road
Lived a man named William Bloat;
He had a wife, the curse of his life,
Who always got his goat.
'Til one day at dawn, with her nightdress on
He slit her pretty throat.

With a razor gash he settled her hash
Oh never was crime so quick
But the steady drip on the pillowslip
Of her lifeblood made him sick.
And the pool of gore on the bedroom floor
Grew clotted and cold and thick.

Now he was right glad he had done as he had
As his wife lay there so still
But a sudden awe of the mighty law
Filled his heart with an icy chill.
So to finish the fun so well begun
He resolved himself to kill.

He took the sheet from the wife's cold feet
And twisted it into a rope
And he hanged himself from the pantry shelf,
'Twas an easy end, let's hope.
In the face of death with his latest breath
He said "to hell with the Pope."

Now the strangest turn in this whole concern
Is only just beginning.
He went to Hell, but his wife got well

And is still alive and sinning.
For the razor blade was German made
But the sheet was Belfast linen.

RAYMOND CALVERT (1906–)

Ballad to a Traditional Refrain

Red brick in the suburbs, white horse on the wall,
Eyetalian marbles in the City Hall:
O stranger from England, why stand so aghast?
May the Lord in His mercy be kind to Belfast.

This jewel that houses our hopes and our fears
Was knocked up from the swamp in the last hundred years;
But the last shall be first and the first shall be last:
May the Lord in His mercy be kind to Belfast.

We swore by King William there'd never been seen
An All-Irish Parliament at College Green,
So at Stormont we're nailing the flag to the mast:
May the Lord in His mercy be kind to Belfast.

O the bricks they will bleed and the rain it will weep,
And the damp Lagan fog lull the city to sleep;
It's to hell with the future and live on the past:
May the Lord in His mercy be kind to Belfast.

MAURICE CRAIG (1919–)

Let Us Be Merry Before We Go

If sadly thinking, with spirits sinking,
    Could, more than drinking, my cares compose,
A cure for sorrow from sighs I'd borrow,
    And hope to-morrow would end my woes.
But as in wailing there's nought availing,
    And Death unfailing will strike the blow,
Then for that reason, and for a season,
    Let us be merry before we go.

To joy a stranger, a wayworn ranger,
    In ev'ry danger my course I've run;
Now hope all ending, and death befriending,
    His last aid lending, my cares are done.
No more a rover, or hapless lover,
    My griefs are over—my glass runs low;
Then for that reason, and for a season,
    Let us be merry before we go.

JOHN PHILPOT CURRAN (1750–1817)

The Parting Glass

O, all the money e'er I had,
I spent it in good company.
And all the harm that ever I've done,
Alas it was to none but me.
And all I've done for want of wit
To mem'ry now I can't recall,
So fill to me the parting glass,
Good night and joy be with you all.

O, all the comrades e'er I had,
They're sorry for my going away,
And all the sweethearts e'er I had,
They'd wished me one more day to stay,
But since it falls unto my lot,
That I should rise and you should not,
I gently rise and softly call,
Good night and joy be with you all.

If I had money enough to spend,
And leisure time to sit awhile,
There is a fair maid in this town,
That sorely has my heart beguiled.
Her rosy cheeks and ruby lips,
I own, she has my heart in thrall,
Then fill to me the parting glass,
Good night and joy be with you all.

TRADITIONAL (17TH CENTURY)

Endpiece

The bells of hell,
Go ting-a-ling-a-ling,
For you but not for me,
Oh death, where is thy sting-a-ling-a-ling?
Or grave thy victory?
If you meet the undertaker,
Or the young man from the Pru,
Get a pint with what's left over,
Now I'll say good-bye to you.

BRENDAN BEHAN (1923–1964)

NOTES TO THE POEMS

Epigraph: Zozimus, or Michael Moran (1794–1846), was a blind Dublin street rhymer and reciter described by W. B. Yeats as "the last gleeman." Blackpits and the Coombe were slum neighborhoods in Dublin.

The Dawning of the Day: Born in Derry and raised in Co. Cork, Edward Walsh worked as a hedge-schoolmaster, a teacher in the National School system, a journalist, and an editor. His *Irish Popular Songs* of 1847 anthologized songs in Irish with metrical translations by Walsh. Lough Lene, where this, his best-known poem, is set can be found in Co. Westmeath.

The Colleen Rue: In English, "the red-headed girl." "Raygions," in the final line, is a dialect spelling of "regions." With its flamboyant display of classical allusions and its use of Gaelic rhyming patterns in English, this poem is typical of the work of the hedge-schoolmaster poets of the late eighteenth and early nineteenth centuries. Hedge schools arose throughout the Irish countryside in response to the Penal Laws of the early eighteenth century, which forbade Roman Catholics to teach school. They were illegal schools often run by a single teacher, or master, and they took their name from the fact that they were often taught outdoors, in the shadow of a hedge. As with most poems and songs in the popular tradition, this one is found in numerous versions and variants, some of them referring to the "colleen fionn," or fair-haired girl. This version is taken from Paddy Tunney's *The Stone Fiddle*.

A Vision: Aodhagan O'Rathaille was one of the last great poets of the Gaelic tradition that finally collapsed after the defeat of King James II at the Battle of the Boyne in 1690. O'Rathaille was from the Sliabh Luachra district near Killarney, an area extremely rich in Irish language poetry and still a center of traditional music. *A Vision*—or, in Irish, *Gile na gile*, literally "brightness of brightness"—is an *aisling*, or dream-vision, a type of poem common in Gaelic poetry in which the poet, wandering at dawn, encounters a beautiful woman, the personification of Ireland. The poem records the poet's disappointed hope for the restoration of a sympathetic Irish ruler. The translator of this version is James Clarence Mangan (1803–1849), one of the foremost Irish poets of the nineteenth century.

The Old Triangle: This song opens and recurs throughout Brendan Behan's play *The Quare Fellow* (1954/56), based on the time he served in Mountjoy Jail, which established his reputation as a playwright of boisterous and obstreperous brilliance. On its London premiere in 1956,

Kenneth Tynan wrote: "The English hoard words like misers; the Irish spend them like sailors; and in Brendan Behan's new play language is out on a spree, ribald, dauntless and spoiling for a fight. In itself, of course, this is scarcely amazing. It is Ireland's sacred duty to send over, every few years, a playwright to save the English theatre from inarticulate glumness." The song has fully entered the popular tradition. "Lag" is slang for a convict, "screw" is slang for a warden.

The Mantle So Green: The beautiful woman with her green mantle, or cloak, whom the poet meets on a morning walk through the fields is the personification of Ireland familiar from the *aisling*. And yet she is also a particular girl named Nancy who is pining for a particular lover, William O'Reilly, who was among the many Irishmen to fight with Wellington's armies in the Battle of Waterloo (June 18, 1815), at which Napoleon Bonaparte suffered his final defeat.

Going to Mass Last Sunday: Donagh MacDonagh, the son of poet and patriot Thomas MacDonagh (see "Thomas MacDonagh" by Francis Ledwidge, p. 103), was a poet, broadcaster, and playwright best remembered for his verse comedy *Happy As Larry*.

The Fiddler of Dooney: Dooney, Kilvarnet, and Mocharabuiee are in Co. Sligo, where W. B. Yeats spent much of his childhood. Yeats, a member of the Protestant Ascendancy, the class that ruled and controlled Ireland from the seventeenth century until the early twentieth century, was fascinated by the traditions and customs of the largely Catholic rural peasantry. This is one of the many instances in Yeats's writing in which he adapted the Irish ballad tradition to his own uses.

The Little Door: This short poem is one of the many stray pieces of verse that survive in the Irish language tradition. Benedict Kiely, one of Ireland's most distinguished living writers, found this quatrain in the Donegal *gaeltacht*, or Irish-speaking district, and made the fine translation given here.

The Forsaken Soldier: Hudie Devaney, a native of Ranafast, in the Donegal *gaeltacht*, is one of the most accomplished singers of traditional songs in Irish. This translation of his "An Saighdiuir Treigthe" is made by Paddy Tunney, an equally accomplished singer and the author of *The Stone Fiddle: My Way to Traditional Song*. Hurling, referred to in the second verse, is an Irish sport played with a stick, or "hurley," and a small ball, or "sliothar." Similar to hockey, it is Europe's oldest field sport.

The Emigrant's Letter: Percy French, one of Ireland's most popular and prolific songwriters, wrote this song on board an ocean liner headed to

America after overhearing a remark made by a departing Donegal emigrant.

The Small Towns of Ireland: John Betjeman, one of the most popular English poets of the century, lived in Ireland from 1941–43. Suspected by the IRA of being a spy, a plot to assassinate him was derailed by an IRA officer who admired his poetry. In this poem, Betjeman records the effects of the transfer of political and commercial power in Ireland from the Protestant Ascendancy to the class of Catholic merchants and farmers. A "glebe house" is a parson's residence; a "phaeton" is a light carriage drawn by one or a pair of horses; the "heroes of brave Ninety-Eight" were the United Irishmen and their followers who took part in a 1798 rebellion against British rule in Ireland. The note at the head of the poem is Betjeman's own.

Brian O'Linn: There are numerous versions of this song that records the adventures of the ever-resourceful Brian O'Linn, including one that occurs in Dion Boucicault's play *The Colleen Bawn*. "The tin" is slang for money; "nate" is a dialect spelling for "neat."

My Grief on the Sea: Douglas Hyde, founder of the Gaelic League and the first president of Ireland, gave this version of a folk poem, originally collected from an old Roscommon peasant woman named Biddy Crummy, in his *Love Songs of Connacht* (1893). As Declan Kiberd notes in his study *Irish Classics*, the poem is a kind of reverse *aisling*, in which a young woman is visited by a dream-vision of her beloved. Leinster is one of the four ancient provinces into which Ireland is divided—the others are Ulster, Connaught, and Munster, where Co. Clare is located.

The Brewer's Man: L. A. G. Strong was born in England, the son of Irish parents. This poem was a favorite of the Welsh poet Dylan Thomas. "Quay," pronounced "key," is a wharf or river embankment.

The Homeward Bound: Thomas D'Arcy McGee was born in Co. Louth, was involved in the Young Ireland Movement and rebellion of 1848, twice emigrated to North America, and finished his life as a Cabinet member in the government of Canada. Cape Clear, Kinsale, Ardigna Bay, and Tramore are on the coastline of West Cork.

The Drynán Dhun: Robert Dwyer Joyce, born in Co. Limerick, is best known as the author of "The Wind That Shakes the Barley." The "drynán dhun" of the title is Irish for the blackthorn or sloe bush. The "rath of the fairy," or fairy fort, refers to the hoary, or ancient, Celtic stone ruins that dot the rural Irish landscape.

On Raglan Road: Patrick Kavanagh, born in Inishkeen, Co. Monaghan, is widely regarded as one of the finer Irish poets of the twentieth century. This poem, written to be sung to the tune of "The Dawning of the Day" (see Edward Walsh poem), records Kavanagh's unrequited love for a young Dublin woman. Raglan Road is in Dublin, not far from where Kavanagh lived for many years; Grafton Street is the main commercial thoroughfare in central Dublin City.

To Inishkea: Katherine Tynan-Hinkson, a friend of Yeats and an astonishingly prolific writer, was born in Dublin and lived for many years in Co. Mayo, where Inishkea and Arran Island are found.

The Mountain Streams Where the Moorcocks Crow: This traditional song is given by Paddy Tunney in his *Stone Fiddle*, where he provides a fine and moving account of the way songs and poems are passed down from one generation to the next. A "moor," or bog, is a field of open wasteland often covered with heather; a "moorcock" is a male moorfowl or red grouse.

From Galway to Graceland: Richard Thompson, born in London in 1949, is a folk and rock guitarist and was a founding member of Fairport Convention. He has also recorded with Linda Thompson and is currently a solo performer. This song, like John Betjeman's "The Small Towns of Ireland," is an instance of a sympathetic English intervention into the Irish ballad tradition.

The Fairies: William Allingham was described by the young W. B. Yeats as his "master in Irish verse." The poem, Allingham's best-known work, refers to the "fairy" or "gentle folk" thought to populate the Irish landscape, to the King and Queen of the Fairies, and to their supposed habit of stealing away children. Columbkill, Slieve League, and the Rosses are in Donegal, where Allingham was born.

The Hill of Killenarden: Charles Graham Halpine, like Thomas D'Arcy McGee, was involved in the Young Ireland Movement and rebellion of 1848. He emigrated to America, where, during the Civil War, he rose to the rank of brigadier general in the Union Army and was involved in raising the first black regiment. Killenarden is in Co. Dublin.

Master McGrath: Master McGrath (1866–1871), a black and white greyhound owned by Lord Lurgan, was the three-time winner of the Waterloo Cup at Altcar in England and was a national hero of sorts in his native Ireland. He visited Queen Victoria at Windsor Castle. An autopsy performed at his death revealed that his heart was as big as a man's. In Ireland, "McGrath" is pronounced "McGraw."

O'Mahony's Lament: John O'Mahony (1816–1877) took part in the failed rebellion of 1848 led by William Smith O'Brien. In exile in America, he founded the Fenian Brotherhood, an international organization committed to the overthrow of British rule in Ireland. Douglas Hyde wrote this poem from the perspective of O'Mahony's last years in New York City, where he died in poverty.

An Irishman's Dream: This song is from the 1916 musical *Broadway and Buttermilk* by John J. O'Brien, Al Dubin, and Rennie Cormack. Irish-American performers and themes were a staple of the American music-hall tradition, and this song is a typical instance of a sentimental and comical "stage Irish" song.

The Mountains of Mourne: The Mourne Mountains are in Co. Down, a long way, or so it seemed to Percy French, from the dazzling life of fashionable London.

The Broad Majestic Shannon: Shane MacGowan, singer and songwriter for the London-based punk and Irish folk band the Pogues and later for the Popes, has been described by the *All Music Guide* as "a transcendent singer/songwriter and two-fisted gutter poet whose notorious drunken behavior, rotten teeth and drug-fueled excesses threatened to eclipse his reputation as a performer." Glenveagh is in Co. Donegal; Finnoe and Shinrone are in Co. Tipperary, through which the broad, majestic River Shannon flows.

The County of Mayo: Little is known of Thomas Lavelle, the author of the Irish language original of this translation by George Fox (1809–1880). Lavelle must have known something of Patrick Loughlin, Brian Duff, Colonel Hugh McGrady, and the other long-dead and forgotten inhabitants of Irrul, in Co. Mayo. Jack B. Yeats, the foremost Irish painter of the twentieth century and the brother of the poet W. B. Yeats, took the title of his novel *Sailing, Sailing Swiftly* from this poem.

The Wee Lassie's First Luve: This is a ballad from Co. Down and reflects the accent found there. The first two lines might be given in standard English as "I cannot hear his name and hide / My thought with any art." One of the pleasures of reading a poem in dialect is trying to figure out what it means, though it probably would not hurt to know that "dinnae" means "do not"; "cannae" means "cannot"; "agley" means "awry or askew"; "een" means "eyes"; and "thole" means "bear or endure."

The Street Ballad-Singer's Song: Jeremiah O'Donovan Rossa's short ballad, which has not been published previously, was discovered by Ted O'Reilly on the flyleaf of a copy of *The Felon's Track* in the library of the

American Irish Historical Society in New York. It is in Rossa's hand and is dated "Sept. 5 1912." Next to the title is a note identifying the subject as Daniel O'Connell, the great nineteenth-century Irish political leader known as the Liberator. O'Connell (1775–1847) was the most effective politician in early-nineteenth-century Ireland. He was centrally responsible for Catholic Emancipation from the Penal Laws and led the vastly popular though ultimately unsuccessful movement to repeal the Act of Union that bound Ireland to Great Britain. There is a further note on that flyleaf, in a different hand, that reads "Rossa wrote the above during his last long illness; he died June 29, 1915 and had been confined to bed for five years."

Street Ballad: William Orr, a prosperous Presbyterian farmer, was hanged in Carrickfergus, Co. Antrim, on October 14, 1797 for allegedly administering the oath of the United Irishmen to two English soldiers. The United Irishmen, led by Theobald Wolfe Tone, were a nondenominational group committed to following the model of the American Revolution and liberating Ireland from British rule. They were the prime movers behind the failed rebellion of 1798.

Rody McCorley: This is another story of a nationalist "martyr" executed for participating in the rebellion of 1798. Toome, Duneane, Drumaul, Ballyscullion, and Ballymena are places in Co. Antrim where Rody McCorley, like William Orr before him, was hanged for participating in the United Irishmen conspiracy against the British crown. Ethna Carberry's version on the same theme is among the best known Irish traditional songs.

The Wild Colonial Boy: This Australian song is one of many in the Irish tradition that celebrate the lives and deaths of outlaws. There was a considerable exportation of Irish men and women, many of them convicts, to Australia in the late eighteenth and early nineteenth centuries. Castlemaine, where Jack Duggan was born and raised, is in Co. Kerry.

The Silence of Unlaboured Fields: This poem by Joseph Campbell of Co. Down laments the depopulation of rural Ireland in the aftermath of the Great Famine (1845–1850) and the pattern of massive emigration it established. During the period of the Famine, it is estimated that the population of Ireland, through death and emigration. declined from 8 million to 5 million persons.

The Workman's Friend: This poem, attributed to "Jem Casey," is part of Flann O'Brien's comic novel *At Swim-Two-Birds*. Jem Casey is described by another character in the novel as the "one man that can write pomes that you can read all day and all night and keep reading them to your heart's content, stuff you'd never tire of. Pomes written down by a man that is one of ourselves and written down for ourselves to read." Flann O'Brien was one of the many pseudonyms used by the novelist and newsprint artist Brian O'Nolan (1911–1966). A "pint of plain" refers to plain porter, a drink cheaper than stout; "rashers" are bacon.

To My Son in Americay: This parody of the broadside tradition was sent to me by its author, a fiction writer and poet and former librarian of the National Library of Ireland. The "first economical plan" refers to the Irish government's eventually successful endeavor to reverse the pattern of emigration that began before the Great Famine and continued until the 1990s. Cobh, in Co. Cork, was the harbor from which many Irish emigrant ships departed. The G.P.O. is the General Post Office.

The Man of the North Countrie: Garryowen is in Co. Limerick in the south of Ireland, Ballybay is in Co. Monaghan in the north. The poem refers to traditional rivalries among the provinces and counties of Ireland. The device by which a male poet writes in a female voice has been present for centuries in Irish poetry.

The Low-Back'd Car: Samuel Lover was a popular and prolific Irish novelist and versifier. A low-back'd car was an unfashionable type of carriage; "forninst" means "facing," or "opposite."

She Is Far from the Land: Thomas Moore is the author of many of the most popular "popular" songs in the Irish popular song tradition. This song is about Sarah Curran, the daughter of John Philpot Curran (see "Let Us Be Merry Before We Go," p. 142), who was engaged to be married to Robert Emmet at the time he was executed for planning a rebellion against the Crown in 1803. After Emmet's execution she married a soldier named Robert Sturgeon and moved to Sicily, where Moore imagines her.

If I Was a Blackbird: This lovely song finds its echo in Padraic Colum's "She Moved through the Fair." Donnybrook Fair, on the outskirts of Dublin, was a great annual gathering noted for its rowdiness.

The Croppy Boy: This well-known ballad of the 1798 rising is one of two distinct versions. The Croppy Boys were so-called because they cropped their hair short like the French revolutionaries they emulated. Lord Cornwallis, who led the British Army defeated in the American Revolution, was more successful at putting down this rebellion in Ireland.

The New Irish Girl: This simple love song from the late eighteenth century draws on some motifs from the *aisling* tradition, but the pain it expresses is wholly personal rather than political.

Kilcash: Kilcash was the great house of the Butler family, a landed Catholic family, near Clonmel, Co. Tipperary. This poem records the family's decline from power and prominence and the consequent loss of their patronage by poets and musicians of the beleaguered Gaelic tradition. The timber from Kilcash was sold as a last bid for solvency at the end of the eighteenth century, and it is from this time that the Irish-language original poem dates.

The Outlaw of Loch Lene: This moonshiner's lament, translated from the Irish by Jeremiah Joseph Callanan, is set on the shores of the same lake in Co. Westmeath where Edward Walsh greeted "the dawning of the day." Padraic Colum notes how Callanan captures the "wavering rhythm" of the Irish-language original.

Moorloch Mary: Ethna Carbery was the pseudonym of Anna MacManus, a native of Co. Antrim and the wife of the writer and folklorist Seamus MacManus. Moorloch, now customarily spelled Moorlough, is in Co. Tyrone. Astórin, a term of endearment, means "my little treasure." The berries of the rowan tree, or the mountain ash, are as red as the lips of a pretty girl. Derry is a county in Ulster.

A Glass of Beer: James Stephens is best remembered as the author of the comic fantasia *The Crock of Gold*. He was born in the same city on the same day in the same year as his friend James Joyce, who ascribed mystical import to this coincidence. A gill is an old form of liquid measurement, roughly equivalent to a quarter-pint.

The Blind Traveller: Translated by Alf MacLochlainn from the traditional poem "An radaire dall," a rare instance of overtly feminist writing in early Irish literature. This poem probably dates from the late eighteenth or early nineteenth century. Tyrone and Mayo are in the north and west of Ireland, respectively, Meath is in the center. The tinkers, or "travellers," were Irish Gypsies who traveled the country often making a living trading horses and mending pots and pans.

Me an' Me Da: The Rev. William Marshall of Sixmilecross was born in Omagh, Co. Tyrone, near Drumlister, Carmin, Cullentra, and Mullaslin. "Clabber" or "bonnyclabber" is thick, curdled milk. For "deil" read "devil"; for "claner" read "cleaner"; for "rared" read "reared"; for "weemin" read "women"; for "kiffled" read "switched"; for "forrit" read "forth"; for "gaol dure" read "jail door"; and so on. It's a lot more fun to figure these out for oneself, but that should be a start.

The Galbally Farmer: This poem records the sorry lot of a "spalpeen" or hired laborer, one of the many migrant workers who would seek work at the hiring fairs that were a feature of rural Irish life from the seventeenth century up until the 1940s. Michaelmas, the Feast of St. Michael and All Angels, is on September 29, near the autumnal equinox, at the end of the harvest; in more generous households than Darby O'Leary's it was celebrated with a feast that included a special loaf of Michaelmas bread. Galbally, a fine place really, is in Co. Limerick. The places named in the great flurry that fills the last stanza of this song are found across the length and breadth of Ireland.

An Elegy on the Death of a Mad Dog: Oliver Goldsmith was born in Co. Roscommon, in the lush midlands of Ireland, where his famous poem "The Deserted Village" is set. Islington is in London, where Goldsmith spent most of his professional career.

The Ould Orange Flute: The Orange Order is a worldwide Protestant fraternity with a particularly strong following in Northern Ireland. Members and supporters of the Order march each year on July 12 to commemorate the victory of William of Orange, later William III of England, over the Catholic, or "Papish," King James II at the Battle of the Boyne in 1690. "Paters and Aves" would be "Our Fathers and Hail Marys" said by Catholics praying the Rosary on their "brown beads." "The Protestant Boys," "Kick the Pope," "The Boyne Water," and "Croppies Lie Down" are triumphalist Orange songs.

The Winding Banks of Erne: Ballyshannon is in Co. Donegal, where the River Erne meets the sea. "Shanachus" or "seincheas" is Irish for old native stories and lore. A "rath" is a fairy-fort or earthwork. This poem, like many in this collection, exemplifies the Irish love of place-names and place-lore, or *dinnseanchas*, a theme and fascination that was carried over from the Gaelic tradition into Irish writing in English.

Love Is Pleasing: As in "My Grief on the Sea" and "If I Was a Blackbird" and many other songs and poems in the Irish popular tradition, the female narrative voice seems to bring with it a greater directness and simplicity. There are many versions of this song, and some of the verses given here appear in other songs such as "Weela Weela Walla" and "The Butcher Boy."

Thomas MacDonagh: Francis Ledwidge was killed in Belgium during the First World War. His poem is a lament for Thomas MacDonagh, a poet and revolutionary who was executed by the British Army for his leadership role in the Easter Rising of 1916.

The Convict of Clonmel: This traditional lament from the mid-eighteenth century was translated from the Irish by Cork poet Jeremiah Joseph Callanan (see "The Outlaw of Loch Lene," p. 86). Clonmala, Cluain Meala, or Clonmel means "Honey Meadow" and is in Co. Tipperary.

The Lambs on the Green Hills: The common theme of the disappointed suitor, given here with its strange, lyrical, irrelevant opening stanza, is revisited by Shane MacGowan in "A Pair of Brown Eyes."

A White Rose: John Boyle O'Reilly was born in Drogheda, Co. Louth. He survived a death sentence for his involvement in the 1848 rebellion, as well as an escape from an Australian prison labor camp, and eventually settled in Boston, where he was for many years editor of *The Pilot*, a paper he made notable for its championing of the rights of African Americans, Jews, and American Indians.

My Love Is Like the Sun: The title is in distinct contrast to Shakespeare's Dark Lady, whose eyes are "nothing like the sun." The Curragh of Kildare is the site of the Ireland's foremost race-course.

The Spanish Man: F. R. Higgins was born in Foxford, Co. Mayo. Claddagh is a fishing village near Galway on the Corrib River. "Pampooties" are a kind of woolen shoe or slipper once common in the West of Ireland.

Oh! Breathe Not His Name: This is Thomas Moore's elegy for renowned Irish patriot Robert Emmet (1778–1803), who was hanged in Dublin for attempting to lead a rebellion against the British Crown, one of the last gasps of the United Irishman movement. At the time of his execution, in his famous speech from the dock, Emmet declared, "When my country takes her place among the nations of the earth, then shall my character be vindicated, then may my epitaph be written."

Les Silhouettes: Oscar Fingal O'Flahertie Wills Wilde, a native of Dublin, is known for his comic plays, his witticisms, and his imprisonment for perjury in a libel trial that he brought against the father of his lover, Alfred Douglas, who had called him a sodomite or, more particularly, a "somdomite." Wilde memorialized his term behind bars in "The Ballad of Reading Gaol," another literary work that draws upon the popular broadside ballad tradition.

Here's to the Maiden: Richard Brinsley Sheridan was born in Dublin. This song is from his most popular play, *The School for Scandal*. "Quean" is a word for a prostitute. A "bumper," or "bombard," is a drinking vessel filled to the brim.

The Spanish Lady: This song has fully passed into the popular tradition, is found in numerous versions, and is rarely attributed to its true author, Joseph Campbell. The Poddle is an underground river in the heart of Dublin; the Hellfire Club in the Dublin Hills was a gathering place for aristocratic rakes in the eighteenth century; a "sizar" was a scholarship student at Trinity College; "mott" was Dublin slang for girlfriend; James Napper Tandy (1740–1803) was a Dublin-born United Irishman who took part in an abortive, French-assisted invasion of Ireland in 1798.

Whiskey in Me Tay: Crossmaglen—where our humble narrator was tricked into drunkenness and, in the way of these things, found himself in a fight—is in Co. Armagh, Carrickmacross and Ballybay are in Co. Monaghan, and Shercock is in Co. Cavan, all counties in the "Border Country" of South Ulster.

Epigrams: These epigrams, translated from the Irish by the poet Maire MacEntee, are from Co. Kerry. They would likely have originated in the seventeenth century, in the period after the Flight of the Earls (1607), when the old Gaelic order was in its terminal decline. They represent a folk version of the same bitter sentiments treated by O'Rathaille in his *aisling* (see "A Vision," p. 21).

Sweet Omagh Town: Omagh, birthplace of Benedict Kiely and the Rev. William Marshall, is in Co. Tyrone.

The Old Bog Road: Teresa Brayton was born in Kilbrook, Co. Kildare, and died there, after having lived for many years in the United States.

She Moved through the Fair: This poem by Padraic Colum echoes the themes of Douglas Hyde's translation "My Grief on the Sea" with a reversal of genders. At a party after the P.E.N. conference in New York in 1965, the poet stood on the coffee table in my parents' apartment and began to recite this lovely piece, only to be interrupted by my father's uncle Dan, who had poems of his own that he wanted to share with the company.

The Three Jolly Pigeons: This song is from Goldsmith's play *She Stoops to Conquer, or The Mistakes of a Night* (1773). A British "crown" was a silver coin worth five shillings; a "jorum" is a large drinking bowl.

A Pair of Brown Eyes: In a way that moves between direct narrative and a more imagistic presentation, this song tells the story of a wounded soldier returned from the war to find his beloved gone to another man. There are at least two distinct songs called "Where the Water Lilies Grow," one by Arthur Percy from 1874 and one by Harry Green published in 1875. Ray Lynam and Philomena Begley, Ireland's queen of country music, are on the jukebox singing "My Elusive Dreams," a 1967 song written by Curly Putnam and Billy Sherrill and more famously recorded by, among others, George Jones and Tammy Wynette, Nancy Sinatra, and Tom Jones.

Ringsend: Oliver St. John Gogarty was a poet, a physician, and a noted Dublin wit. He served unwillingly as the model for James Joyce's plump Buck Mulligan in *Ulysses*, and his loveliest line, the last line of "Ringsend," was parodied by Joyce, who referred to his former friend's "lapsang, unsaleable, whiskery tea." In 1939, following his loss as a defendant in a libel case in which Samuel Beckett testified against him, Gogarty moved to the United States, where he spent most of his last two decades. Ringsend is a working-class neighborhood in Dublin quite unlike the center of Dublin City in which Gogarty actually lived.

The Night Before Larry Was Stretched: This is a Dublin street poem of the mid-eighteenth century. It is about a visit paid to a condemned man by his pals the night before he is to be hanged, or "stretched." They bring whiskey, cards, and candles for his wake, which they've pawned their clothes to buy. The last line of each stanza, which falls outside the rhyme scheme, was meant to be spoken rather than sung. Jack Ketch was a noted Dublin hangman; Kilmainham was a jail.

Song of the Ghost: This poem by Alfred Percival Graves, Gaelic scholar and father of the poet Robert Graves, was included by W. B. Yeats in his *Fairy and Folk Tales of the Irish Peasantry* (1888). A "bower" is a bedroom; a "bier" is a frame on which a corpse is laid out to be carried to the grave.

The Ballad of William Bloat: This piece by Raymond Calvert is usually described as a traditional ballad, which, in the way of these things, it has become. It was written for a Queen's University Dramatic Society cast party in 1926. The Shankill Road is the main artery of a hard-line Unionist neighborhood in Belfast, a city noted for its linen-works.

Ballad to a Traditional Refrain: Maurice Craig is a writer and a scholar now living in Dublin. The white horse on the wall belongs to King William of Orange, who defeated the Catholic armies of James II at the Battle of the Boyne in 1690, a favorite scene for urban muralists in Belfast's Protestant working-class neighborhoods. College Green is in Dublin. Stormont Castle in Belfast was the seat of the government of Northern Ireland until 1974, when the province reverted to Direct Rule by the government of the United Kingdom. The River Lagan runs through Belfast.

Let Us Be Merry Before We Go: John Philpot Curran, a statesman and trial lawyer who defended some of the United Irishmen after the 1798 rebellion, was the father of Robert Emmet's beloved, Sarah Curran (see "She Is Far from the Land," p. 77).

The Parting Glass: At the end of a party in Dublin in 1996, Ben Kiely asked those assembled, "Have you ever heard me sing 'The Parting Glass'?"—to which a beautiful woman named Frances Daly answered, "Moments ago, Ben."

Endpiece: This farewell is from the end of Brendan Behan's second great play *The Hostage* (1958). "O death, where is thy sting? O grave, where is thy victory set?" is a question asked also in the First Book of the Corinthians. The "young man from the Pru" presumably works for the Prudential Life Insurance Company.

CREDITS

"The Old Triangle": Reprinted from *The Quare Fellow* with permission of Grove/Atlantic Inc. and the Behan Estate. *The Quare Fellow* © 1956 by Brendan Behan and Theatre Workshop.

"Going to Mass Last Sunday": Reprinted from Benedict Kiely's *And As I Rode by Granard Moat*, by permission of the publisher, Lilliput Press of Dublin, Ireland.

"The Fiddler of Dooney": Reprinted with the permission of Scribner, an imprint of Simon & Schuster Adult Publishing Group, from *The Collected Works of W. B. Yeats, Volume I: The Poems, Revised*, edited by Richard J. Finneran. (New York: Scribner, 1997).

"The Little Door": Reprinted by permission of the translator, Benedict Kiely.

"The Forsaken Soldier": Reprinted from Benedict Kiely's *And As I Rode by Granard Moat*, by permission of the publisher, Lilliput Press of Dublin, Ireland.

"The Small Towns of Ireland": Reprinted from John Betjeman's *Collected Poems*, by permission of John Murray (Publishers) Ltd., and the estate of John Betjeman.

"On Raglan Road": Reprinted from Patrick Kavanagh's *Collected Poems* by permission of Devin-Adair Company and Katherine Kavanagh.

"From Galway to Graceland": By Richard Thompson, © 1993 Beeswing Music (BMI)/Administered by BUG. All Rights Reserved. Used by Permission.

"The Workman's Friend": From *At Swim-Two-Birds* by Flann O'Brien, copyright © 1939 by Brian O'Nolan, copyright renewed © 1967 by Evelyn O'Nolan. Reprinted by permission of Brandt and Hochman Literary Agents, Inc.

"To My Son in Americay": Reprinted by permission of the author.

"Kilcash": Reprinted by permission of PFD on behalf of the Estate of Frank O'Connor. © 1950, Frank O'Connor.

ACKNOWLEDGMENTS

I first heard many of the poems and songs in this collection when I was a child, sung by my mother or read or recited by my father. Most of the rest I heard from Ben Kiely—novelist, story writer, and unparalleled raconteur—to whom this book is dedicated. Many of them are given or quoted in Ben's books, particularly *And As I Rode by Granard Moat, All the Way to Bantry Bay,* and *Dublin.* Other books also of great help to me in compiling this collection were: *The Stone Fiddle* by Paddy Tunney and *Irish Street Ballads* and *More Irish Street Ballads* by Colm O'Lochlainn. I am indebted for personal recommendations to Alf MacLochlainn, Colum McCann, and Eoin O'Brien. I am especially grateful to Ted O'Reilly for his invaluable assistance.